M000003549

Math and Science Activities

Join us on the web at

EarlyChildEd.delmar.com

Math and Science Activities

Jennifer M. Johnson

THOMSON
™
DELMAR LEARNING

Australia • Canada • Mexico • Singapore • Spain • United Kingdom • United States

COPYRIGHT © 2007 Thomson Delmar Learning, a part of The Thomson Corporation.
Thomson, the Star logo, and Delmar Learning are trademarks used herein under license.

Printed in the United States
1 2 3 4 5 xxx 10 09 08 07 06

For more information contact Thomson Delmar Learning, Executive Woods, 5 Maxwell
Drive, Clifton Park, NY 12065-2919

Or find us on the World Wide Web at http://www.delmarlearning.com, or
www.earlychilded.delmar.com

ALL RIGHTS RESERVED. No part of this work covered by the copyright hereon may be
reproduced or used in any form or by any means—graphic, electronic, or mechanical,
including photocopying, recording, taping, Web distribution or information storage and
retrieval systems—without written permission of the publisher.

For permission to use material from this text or product, contact us by
Tel   (800) 730-2214
Fax   (800) 730-2215
www.thomsonrights.com

ISBN-10: 1-4180-0156-2
ISBN-13: 978-1-4180-0156-8

Library of Congress Catalog Card Number: 2006003499

NOTICE TO THE READER

The authors and Thomson Delmar Learning affirm that the Web site URLs referenced
herein were accurate at the time of printing. However, due to the fluid nature of the
Internet, we cannot guarantee their accuracy for the life of the edition.

TABLE OF CONTENTS

Introduction   vii

Reflections for Growing Teachers   1

Tips for Success   5

Getting Started   8

Developmental Milestones by Age   11

Developmental Milestones by Skill   28

Play Materials for Children   42

Observation and Assessment   56

Curriculum and Lesson Plans   62

Books for Children   71

Books   74

Developmentally Appropriate Practice   81

Guidelines for Developmentally Appropriate Practice   83

Professional Organizations   86

Resources   91

Case Studies   98

Issues and Trends   100

This tool was developed to help you, the budding teacher and/or
child care provider, as you move into your first classroom.
The editors at Thomson Delmar Learning encourage and
appreciate your feedback on this or any of our other products.
Go to www.earlychilded.delmar.com and click on
the "Professional Enhancement series feedback" link to let us know what you think.

INTRODUCTION

Throughout a college program of preparation to become an early childhood educator, students take many courses and read many textbooks. Their knowledge grows, as they accumulate ideas from lectures, reading, experiences, and discussions. When they finish their coursework, graduate, and move into their first teaching positions, students often leave behind some of the books they have used. The hope is, however, that they will take with them the important ideas from their classes and books as they begin their own professional practice.

More experienced colleagues or mentors sometimes support teachers in their first teaching positions, helping them make the transition between college classroom and being responsible for a group of young children. Other times, new teachers are left to travel their own paths, relying on their own resources. Whatever your situation, this professional enhancement guide is designed to provide reminders of what you have learned, as well as resources to help you make sense of and apply that knowledge.

Teachers of young children are under great pressure today. From families, there are the demands for support in their difficult tasks of child-rearing in today's fast-paced and changing world. Some families become so overwhelmed with the tasks of parenting that they seem to leave too much responsibility on the shoulders of teachers and caregivers. From administrators and institutions, there are expectations that sometimes seem overwhelming. Teachers are being held accountable for children's learning in ways unprecedented in even the recent past. Public scrutiny has led to insistence on teaching practices that may seem contrary to the best interests of children or their teachers. New teachers may find themselves caught between the realities of the schools or centers where they find themselves, and their own philosophies and ideals of working with children. When faced with such dilemmas, it is important for these individuals to be able to fall back and reflect on what they know of best practices, renewing their professional determination to make appropriate decisions for children.

These books provide similar tools for that reflection:

- tips for getting off to a great start in your new environment

- information about typical developmental patterns of children from birth through school age

- suggestions for materials that promote development for children from infancy through the primary grades

- tools to assist teachers in observing children and gathering data to help set appropriate goals for individual children

- guides for planning appropriate classroom experiences and sample lesson plans

- tips for introducing children to the joys of literacy

- a summary of the key ideas about Developmentally Appropriate Practice, the process of decision-making that allows teachers to provide optimum environments for children from birth through school age

- resources for teachers for professional development

- ideas for where you can access lists of other resources

- case studies of relevant, realistic situations you may face, as well as best practices for successfully navigating them

- insight into issues and trends facing early childhood educators today

- This book has been designed for usability. The margins have been enlarged to enable use of this space for note taking.

Becoming a teacher is a process of continuing to grow, learn, reflect, and discover through experience. Having these resources may help you along your way. Good luck on your journey!

REFLECTIONS FOR GROWING TEACHERS

Teachers spend most of their time working with young children and their families. During the day, questions and concerns arise and decisions have to be made, meaning teachers must always be reflective about their work. Too often, teachers believe they are too busy to spend time thinking, but experienced professional teachers have learned that reflection sustains their best work. Growing teachers need to regularly take time to consider the questions and concerns that arise from their practice. Some teachers use journals to keep track of the process.

Use these questions to begin your reflection and then add to them with questions from your own experience. Remember, these are not questions to be answered once and forgotten; come back often.

QUESTIONS FOR REFLECTION

This day would have been better if _____

I think I need to know more about _____

One new thing I think I will try this week is _____

The highlight of this week was   _____

The observations this week made me think more about _____

I think my favorite creative activity this year was _____

One area where my teaching is changing is _____

One area where my teaching needs to change is _____

I just do not understand why _____

I loved my job this week when _____

I hated my job this week when _____

One thing I can try to make better next week is _____

The funniest thing I heard a child say this week was _____

The family member I feel most comfortable with is _____

And I think the reason for that is _____

The family member I feel least comfortable with is _____

And I think the reason for that is _____

The biggest gains in learning have been made by _____

And I think that this is because _____

I am working on a bad habit of _____

Has my attitude about teaching changed this year? Why? _____

What have I done lately to spark the children's imagination and creativity? _____

_____

One quote that I like to keep in mind is _____

Dealing with _____ is the most difficult thing I had to face recently because ____

_____

My teaching style has been most influenced by _____

_____

In thinking more about math and science in my curriculum, I believe . . . _____

If I were going to advise a new teacher, the most helpful piece of advice would be

_____

I have been trying to facilitate friendships among the children by _____

I really need to start _____

I used to _____ but now I _____

_____

The child who has helped me learn the most is _____ I learned _____

_____

I have grown in my communication by _____

The best thing I have learned by observing is _____

I still do not understand why _____

One mistake I used to make that I do not make any longer is _____

When next year starts, one thing I will do more of is _____

_____

When next year starts, one thing I will not do is _____

_____

One way I can help my children feel more competent is _____

Something I enjoy that I could share with my class is _____

_____

When children have difficulty sharing, I _____

_____

_____

_____

(Adapted from Nilsen, B. A., (2005). *Week by Week: Documenting the Development of Young Children* (3rd ed.), published by Thomson Delmar Learning.)

TIPS FOR SUCCESS

Remember that you are a role model for the children. They are constantly watching how you dress, what you say, and what you do.

BE A PROFESSIONAL

- Dress conservatively and follow your employer's clothing expectations (which could include wearing closed-toe shoes to be safe and active with children and wearing clean, modest, and comfortable clothing).

- Be prepared and on time.

- Avoid excessive absences.

- Use appropriate language with children and adults.

- Be positive when talking to parents and show that you are forming a positive relationship with their child; "catch children doing something right" and share those accomplishments. Challenges with children can be discussed after you have established trust with the parents.

BE A TEAM PLAYER

- Rely on team members to help you learn the parameters of your new position.

- Don't be afraid to ask questions or for guidance from teammates.

- Show your support and be responsible.

- Step in to do your share of the work; don't expect others to clean up after you.

- Be of assistance to others whenever possible.

- Respect others' ideas and avoid telling them how to do things.

- Strive to balance your ability to make decisions with following the lead of others.

LEARN ABOUT CHILDREN

- Be aware of children's development physically, socially, emotionally, and cognitively.

- Assess children's development and plan curriculum that will enhance it.

- Be aware that children will test you! (Children, especially school age, will expect that you don't know the rules and may try to convince you to let them do things that were not previously allowed.)

- Never hesitate to double-check something with teammates when in doubt.

- Use positive management techniques with children.

MANAGEMENT TECHNIQUES FOR GAINING CHILDREN'S COOPERATION

There are myriad techniques that will help children cooperate. Children need respectful reminders of expectations and adult support in performing to those expectations. Be sure that your expectations are age appropriate and individually appropriate. These techniques are more preventive in nature:

- Use positive phrases and state exactly what you expect children to do. "Stand by the door" is more effective than "Don't go outside until everyone is ready."

- Avoid "no" and "don't." Be clear about what it is you want children to do, not what you don't want them to do.

- Sequence directions using "When-then." For example, "When things are put away where they belong, then we can go outside."

■ Stay close. Merely standing near children can be enough to help them manage behavior. Be aware, however, that if you are talking to another adult, children may act out because they know they do not have your attention.

■ Offer sufficient and appropriate choices. Children need a variety of activities that interest them and that will create opportunities for success.

GETTING STARTED

There is always an array of information to learn when starting in a new position working with children. Use this fill-in-the-blank section to customize this resource book to your specific environment.

What are the school's or center's hours of operation?

On school days: _____

On vacation days: _____

What is the basic daily schedule and what are my responsibilities during each time segment?

_____

_____

_____

_____

_____

_____

What are the procedures for checking children in and out of the program?

_____

_____

Do I call if I have to be absent? Who is my contact?

Name _____

Phone Number _____

What is the dress code for employees?

_____

_____

For what basic health and safety practices will I be responsible? Where are the materials stored for this? (Bleach, gloves, etc.)

Sanitizing tables

_____

_____

_____

Cleaning and maintaining of equipment and materials _____

_____

_____

What are the emergency procedures?

Mildly injured child: _____

_____

_____

_____

Earthquake/Tornado: _____

_____

_____

Fire:

_____

_____

_____

First Aid:

_____

_____

_____

Other:

_____

_____

_____

DEVELOPMENTAL MILESTONES BY AGE

Whether you are working with infants, toddlers, preschoolers, or primary-aged children, a teacher's first requirement is to have knowledge about how children develop and learn. In your college program, you no doubt studied child development. The following is a shortened version of the universal steps most children go through as they develop. Some children will move easily from one step to another, while other children move forward in one area but lag behind in others. Use these milestones as a guide for arranging an environment or planning activities in your room.

Child's name _____ Age _____

Observer _____ Date _____

Developmental Checklist (by six months)

Does the child . . .	Yes	No	Sometimes
Show continued gains in height, weight, and head circumference?	☐	☐	☐
Reach for toys or objects when they are presented?	☐	☐	☐
Begin to roll from stomach to back?	☐	☐	☐
Sit with minimal support?	☐	☐	☐
Transfer objects from one hand to the other?	☐	☐	☐
Raise up on arms, lifting head and chest, when placed on stomach?	☐	☐	☐
Babble, coo, and imitate sounds?	☐	☐	☐
Turn to locate the source of a sound?	☐	☐	☐
Focus on an object and follow its movement vertically and horizontally?	☐	☐	☐
Exhibit a blink reflex?	☐	☐	☐
Enjoy being held and cuddled?	☐	☐	☐
Recognize and respond to familiar faces?	☐	☐	☐
Begin sleeping six to eight hours through the night?	☐	☐	☐
Suck vigorously when it is time to eat?	☐	☐	☐
Enjoy playing in water during bath time?	☐	☐	☐

DEVELOPMENTAL ALERTS

Check with a health care provider or early childhood specialist if, by one month of age, the infant *does not:*

- Show alarm or "startle" responses to loud noise.

- Suck and swallow with ease.

- Show gains in height, weight, and head circumference.

- Grasp with equal strength with both hands.

- Make eye-to-eye contact when awake and being held.

- Become quiet soon after being picked up.

- Roll head from side to side when placed on stomach.

- Express needs and emotions with cries and patterns of vocalizations that can be distinguished from one another.

- Stop crying when picked up and held.

DEVELOPMENTAL ALERTS

Check with a health care provider or early childhood specialist if, by four months of age, the infant *does not:*

- Continue to show steady increases in height, weight, and head circumference.

- Smile in response to the smiles of others (the social smile is a significant developmental milestone).

- Follow a moving object with eyes focusing together.

- Bring hands together over midchest.

- Turn head to locate sounds.

- Begin to raise head and upper body when placed on stomach.

- Reach for objects or familiar persons.

Child's name _____ Age _____

Observer _____ Date _____

Developmental Checklist (by twelve months)

Does the child . . .	Yes	No	Sometimes
Walk with assistance?	☐	☐	☐
Roll a ball in imitation of an adult?	☐	☐	☐
Pick objects up with thumb and forefinger?	☐	☐	☐
Transfer objects from one hand to the other?	☐	☐	☐
Pick up dropped toys?	☐	☐	☐
Look directly at adult's face?	☐	☐	☐
Imitate gestures: peek-a-boo, bye-bye, pat-a-cake?	☐	☐	☐
Find object hidden under a cup?	☐	☐	☐
Feed self crackers (munching, not sucking on them)?	☐	☐	☐
Hold cup with two hands; drink with assistance?	☐	☐	☐
Smile spontaneously?	☐	☐	☐
Pay attention to own name?	☐	☐	☐
Respond to "no"?	☐	☐	☐
Respond differently to strangers and familiar persons?	☐	☐	☐
Respond differently to sounds: vacuum, phone, door?	☐	☐	☐
Look at person who speaks to him or her?	☐	☐	☐
Respond to simple directions accompanied by gestures?	☐	☐	☐
Make several consonant–vowel combination sounds?	☐	☐	☐
Vocalize back to person who has talked to him or her?	☐	☐	☐
Use intonation patterns that sound like scolding, asking, exclaiming?	☐	☐	☐
Say "da-da" or "ma-ma"?	☐	☐	☐

DEVELOPMENTAL ALERTS

Check with a health care provider or early childhood specialist if, by twelve months of age, the infant *does not:*

- Blink when fast-moving objects approach the eyes.
- Begin to cut teeth.
- Imitate simple sounds.
- Follow simple verbal requests: *come, bye-bye.*
- Pull self to a standing position.

Child's name _____   Age _____
Observer _____   Date _____

Developmental Checklist (by two years)

Does the child . . .	Yes	No	Sometimes
Walk alone?	☐	☐	☐
Bend over and pick up toy without falling over?	☐	☐	☐
Seat self in child-size chair? Walk up and down stairs with assistance?	☐	☐	☐
Place several rings on a stick?	☐	☐	☐
Place five pegs in a pegboard?	☐	☐	☐
Turn pages two or three at a time?	☐	☐	☐
Scribble?			
Follow one-step direction involving something familiar:			
"Give me _____." "Show me _____." "Get a _____."?	☐	☐	☐
Match familiar objects?	☐	☐	☐
Use spoon with some spilling?	☐	☐	☐
Drink from cup holding it with one hand, unassisted?	☐	☐	☐
Chew food?	☐	☐	☐
Take off coat, shoe, sock?	☐	☐	☐
Zip and unzip large zipper?	☐	☐	☐
Recognize self in mirror or picture?	☐	☐	☐
Refer to self by name?	☐	☐	☐
Imitate adult behaviors in play—for example, feeds "baby"?	☐	☐	☐
Help put things away?	☐	☐	☐
Respond to specific words by showing what was named: toy, pet, family member?	☐	☐	☐
Ask for desired items by name: (cookie)?	☐	☐	☐
Answer with name of object when asked "What's that"?	☐	☐	☐
Make some two-word statements: "Daddy bye-bye"?	☐	☐	☐

DEVELOPMENTAL ALERTS

Check with a health care provider or early childhood specialist if, by twenty-four months of age, the child *does not*:

- Attempt to talk or repeat words.
- Understand some new words.
- Respond to simple questions with "yes" or "no".

- Walk alone (or with very little help).
- Exhibit a variety of emotions: anger, delight, fear.
- Show interest in pictures.
- Recognize self in mirror.
- Attempt self-feeding: hold own cup to mouth and drink.

Child's name Abbey
Age 3

Observer Erin
Date 4-11-08

Developmental Checklist (by three years)

Does the child . . .	Yes	No	Sometimes
Run well in a forward direction?	☑	☐	☐
Jump in place, two feet together?	☐	☐	☐
Walk on tiptoe?	☐	☐	☐
Throw ball (but without direction or aim)?	☐	☐	☐
Kick ball forward?	☐	☐	☐
String four large beads?	☐	☐	☐
Turn pages in book singly?	☑	☐	☐
Hold crayon: imitate circular, vertical, horizontal strokes?	☑	☐	☐
Match shapes?	☑	☐	☐
Demonstrate number concepts of 1 and 2?	☐	☐	☐
(Can select 1 or 2; can tell if one or two objects.)	☐	☐	☐
Use spoon without spilling?	☐	☐	☐
Drink from a straw?	☐	☐	☐
Put on and take off coat?	☑	☐	☐
Wash and dry hands with some assistance?	☑	☐	☐
Watch other children; play near them; sometimes join in their play?	☑	☐	☐
Defend own possessions?	☑	☐	☐
Use symbols in play—for example, tin pan on head becomes helmet and crate becomes a spaceship?	☐	☐	☐
Respond to "Put _____ in the box," "Take the _____ out of the box"?	☐	☐	☐
Select correct item on request: big versus little; one versus two?	☐	☐	☐
Identify objects by their use: show own shoe when asked, "What do you wear on your feet?"	☐	☐	☐
Ask questions?	☑	☐	☐
Tell about something with functional phrases that carry meaning: "Daddy go airplane. "	☐	☐	☐
"Me hungry now"?	☐	☐	☐

DEVELOPMENTAL ALERTS

Check with a health care provider or early childhood specialist if, by the third birthday, the child *does not:*

- Eat a fairly well-rounded diet, even though amounts are limited.

- Walk confidently with few stumbles or falls; climb steps with help.

- Avoid bumping into objects.

- Carry out simple, two-step directions: "Come to Daddy and bring your book"; express desires; ask questions.

- Point to and name familiar objects; use two- or three-word sentences.

- Enjoy being read to.

- Show interest in playing with other children: watching, perhaps imitating.

- Indicate a beginning interest in toilet training.

- Sort familiar objects according to a single characteristic, such as type, color, or size.

Child's name _____   Age _____

Observer _____   Date _____

Developmental Checklist (by four years)

Does the child . . .	Yes	No	Sometimes
Walk on a line?	☐	☐	☐
Balance on one foot briefly? Hop on one foot?	☐	☐	☐
Jump over an object 6 inches high and land on both feet together?	☐	☐	☐
Throw ball with direction?	☐	☐	☐
Copy circles and *X*s?	☐	☐	☐
Match six colors?	☐	☐	☐
Count to 5?	☐	☐	☐
Pour well from pitcher? Spread butter, jam with knife?	☐	☐	☐
Button, unbutton large buttons?	☐	☐	☐
Know own sex, age, last name?	☐	☐	☐
Use toilet independently and reliably?	☐	☐	☐

Wash and dry hands unassisted?	☐	☐	☐
Listen to stories for at least five minutes?	☐	☐	☐
Draw head of person and at least one other body part?	☐	☐	☐
Play with other children?	☐	☐	☐
Share, take turns (with some assistance)?	☐	☐	☐
Engage in dramatic and pretend play?	☐	☐	☐
Respond appropriately to "Put it beside," "Put it under"?	☐	☐	☐
Respond to two-step directions: "Give me the sweater and put the shoe on the floor"?	☐	☐	☐
Respond by selecting the correct object—for example, hard versus soft object?	☐	☐	☐
Answer "if," "what," and "when" questions?	☐	☐	☐
Answer questions about function: "What are books for"?	☐	☐	☐

DEVELOPMENTAL ALERTS

Check with a health care provider or early childhood specialist if, by the fourth birthday, the child *does not:*

- Have intelligible speech most of the time; have children's hearing checked if there is any reason for concern.

- Understand and follow simple commands and directions.

- State own name and age.

- Enjoy playing near or with other children.

- Use three- to four-word sentences.

- Ask questions.

- Stay with an activity for three or four minutes; play alone several minutes at a time.

- Jump in place without falling.

- Balance on one foot, at least briefly.

- Help with dressing self.

FIVE- TO SEVEN-YEAR-OLDS

- More independent of parents, able to take care of their own physical needs

- Rely upon their peer group for self-esteem, have two or three best friends

- Learn to share and take turns, participate in group games

- Are eager to learn and succeed in school

- Have a sense of duty and develop a conscience

- Are less aggressive and resolve conflicts with words

- Begin to see others' point of view

- Can sustain interest for long periods of time

- Can remember and relate past events

- Have good muscle control and can manage simple tools

- Have a high energy level

Child's name _____   Age _____

Observer _____   Date _____

Developmental Checklist (by five years)

Does the child . . .	Yes	No	Sometimes
Walk backward, heel to toe?	☐	☐	☐
Walk up and down stairs, alternating feet?	☐	☐	☐
Cut on line?	☐	☐	☐
Print some letters?	☐	☐	☐
Point to and name three shapes?	☐	☐	☐
Group common related objects: shoe, sock, and foot: apple, orange, and plum?	☐	☐	☐
Demonstrate number concepts to 4 or 5?	☐	☐	☐
Cut food with a knife: celery, sandwich?	☐	☐	☐
Lace shoes?	☐	☐	☐
Read from story picture book—in other words, tell story by looking at pictures?	☐	☐	☐
Draw a person with three to six body parts?	☐	☐	☐

Play and interact with other children; engage in dramatic play that is close to reality?	☐	☐	☐
Build complex structures with blocks or other building materials?	☐	☐	☐
Respond to simple three-step directions: "Give me the pencil, put the book on the table, and hold the comb in your hand"?	☐	☐	☐
Respond correctly when asked to show penny, nickel, and dime?	☐	☐	☐
Ask "How" questions?	☐	☐	☐
Respond verbally to "Hi" and "How are you"?	☐	☐	☐
Tell about event using past and future tenses?	☐	☐	☐
Use conjunctions to string words and phrases together—for example, "I saw a bear and a zebra and a giraffe at the zoo"?	☐	☐	☐

DEVELOPMENTAL ALERTS

Check with a health care provider or early childhood specialist if, by the fifth birthday, the child *does not:*

■ State own name in full.

■ Recognize simple shapes: circle, square, triangle.

■ Catch a large ball when bounced (have child's vision checked).

■ Speak so as to be understood by strangers (have child's hearing checked).

■ Have good control of posture and movement.

■ Hop on one foot.

■ Appear interested in, and responsive to, surroundings.

■ Respond to statements without constantly asking to have them repeated.

■ Dress self with minimal adult assistance; manage buttons, zippers.

■ Take care of own toilet needs; have good bowel and bladder control with infrequent accidents.

Child's name _____   Age _____

Observer _____   Date _____

Developmental Checklist (by six years)

Does the child . . .	Yes	No	Sometimes
Walk across a balance beam?	☐	☐	☐
Skip with alternating feet?	☐	☐	☐
Hop for several seconds on one foot?	☐	☐	☐
Cut out simple shapes?	☐	☐	☐
Copy own first name?	☐	☐	☐
Show well-established handedness; demonstrate consistent right- or left-handedness?	☐	☐	☐
Sort objects on one or more dimensions: color, shape, or function?	☐	☐	☐
Name most letters and numerals?	☐	☐	☐
Count by rote to 10; know what number comes next?	☐	☐	☐
Dress self completely; tie bows?	☐	☐	☐
Brush teeth unassisted?	☐	☐	☐
Have some concept of clock time in relation to daily schedule?	☐	☐	☐
Cross street safely?	☐	☐	☐
Draw a person with head, trunk, legs, arms, and features; often add clothing details?	☐	☐	☐
Play simple board games?	☐	☐	☐
Engage in cooperative play with other children, involving group decisions, role assignments, rule observance?	☐	☐	☐
Use construction toys, such as Legos®, blocks, to make recognizable structures?	☐	☐	☐
Do fifteen-piece puzzles?	☐	☐	☐
Use all grammatical structures: pronouns, plurals, verb tenses, conjunctions?	☐	☐	☐
Use complex sentences: carry on conversations?	☐	☐	☐

DEVELOPMENTAL ALERTS

Check with a health care provider or early childhood specialist if by the sixth birthday, the child *does not:*

- Alternate feet when walking up and down stairs.
- Speak in a moderate voice; neither too loud, too soft, too high, too low.

- Follow simple directions in stated order: "Please go to the cupboard, get a cup, and bring it to me."
- Use four to five words in acceptable sentence structure.
- Cut on a line with scissors.
- Sit still and listen to an entire short story (five to seven minutes).
- Maintain eye contact when spoken to (unless this is a cultural taboo).
- Play well with other children.
- Perform most self-grooming tasks independently: brush teeth, wash hands and face.

Child's name _____   Age _____
Observer _____   Date _____

Developmental Checklist (by seven years)

Does the child . . .	Yes	No	Sometimes
Concentrate on completing puzzles and board games?	☐	☐	☐
Ask many questions?	☐	☐	☐
Use correct verb tenses, word order, and sentence structure in conversation?	☐	☐	☐
Correctly identify right and left hands?	☐	☐	☐
Make friends easily?	☐	☐	☐
Show some control of anger, using words instead of physical aggression?	☐	☐	☐
Participate in play that requires teamwork and rule observance?	☐	☐	☐
Seek adult approval for efforts?	☐	☐	☐
Enjoy reading and being read to?	☐	☐	☐
Use pencil to write words and numbers?	☐	☐	☐
Sleep undisturbed through the night?	☐	☐	☐
Catch a tennis ball, walk across balance beam, hit ball with bat?	☐	☐	☐
Plan and carry out simple projects with minimal adult help?	☐	☐	☐
Tie own shoes?	☐	☐	☐
Draw pictures with greater detail and sense of proportion?	☐	☐	☐
Care for own personal needs with some adult supervision? Wash hands? Brush teeth? Use toilet? Dress self?	☐	☐	☐
Show some understanding of cause-and-effect concepts?	☐	☐	☐

DEVELOPMENTAL ALERTS

Check with a health care provider or early childhood specialist if, by the seventh birthday, the child *does not:*

- Show signs of ongoing growth: increasing height and weight; continuing motor development, such as running, jumping, balancing.

- Show some interest in reading and trying to reproduce letters, especially own name.

- Follow simple, multiple-step directions: "Finish your book, put it on the shelf, and then get your coat on."

- Follow through with instructions and complete simple tasks: putting dishes in the sink, picking up clothes, finishing a puzzle. *Note:* All children forget. Task incompletion is not a problem unless a child *repeatedly* leaves tasks unfinished.

- Begin to develop alternatives to excessive use of inappropriate behaviors in order to get own way.

- Develop a steady decrease in tension-type behaviors that may have developed with starting school: repeated grimacing or facial tics; eye twitching; grinding of teeth; regressive soiling or wetting; frequent stomachaches; refusing to go to school.

EIGHT- TO TEN-YEAR-OLDS

- Need parental guidance and support for school achievement

- Competition is common

- Pronounced gender differences in interests, same gender cliques formed

- Spend a lot of time in physical game playing

- Academic achievement is important

- Begin to develop moral values, make value judgments about own behavior

- Are aware of the importance of belonging

- Strong gender role conformation

- Begin to think logically and to understand cause and effect

- Use language to communicate ideas and can use abstract words
- Can read but ability varies
- Realize importance of physical skills in determining status among peers

---

Child's name _____   Age _____
Observer _____   Date _____

Developmental Checklist (by eight and nine years)

Does the child . . .	Yes	No	Sometimes
Have energy to play, continuing growth, few illnesses?	☐	☐	☐
Use pencil in a deliberate and controlled manner?	☐	☐	☐
Express relatively complex thoughts in a clear and logical fashion?	☐	☐	☐
Carry out multiple four- to five-step instructions?	☐	☐	☐
Become less easily frustrated with own performance?	☐	☐	☐
Interact and play cooperatively with other children?	☐	☐	☐
Show interest in creative expression—telling stories, jokes, writing, drawing, singing?	☐	☐	☐
Use eating utensils with ease?	☐	☐	☐
Have a good appetite? Show interest in trying new foods?	☐	☐	☐
Know how to tell time?	☐	☐	☐
Have control of bowel and bladder functions?	☐	☐	☐
Participate in some group activities—games, sports, plays?	☐	☐	☐
Want to go to school? Seem disappointed if must miss a day?	☐	☐	☐
Demonstrate beginning skills in reading, writing, and math?	☐	☐	☐
Accept responsibility and complete work independently?	☐	☐	☐
Handle stressful situations without becoming overly upset?	☐	☐	☐

DEVELOPMENTAL ALERTS

Check with a health care provider or early childhood specialist if, by the eighth birthday, the child *does not*:

- Attend to the task at hand; show longer periods of sitting quietly, listening, responding appropriately.
- Follow through on simple instructions.
- Go to school willingly most days (of concern are excessive complaints about stomachaches or headaches when getting ready for school).

- Make friends (observe closely to see if the child plays alone most of the time or withdraws consistently from contact with other children).

- Sleep soundly most nights (frequent and recurring nightmares or bad dreams are usually at a minimum at this age).

- Seem to see or hear adequately at times (squints, rubs eyes excessively, asks frequently to have things repeated).

- Handle stressful situations without undue emotional upset (excessive crying, sleeping or eating disturbances, withdrawal, frequent anxiety).

- Assume responsibility for personal care (dressing, bathing, feeding self) most of the time.

- Show improved motor skills.

DEVELOPMENTAL ALERTS

Check with a health care provider or early childhood specialist if, by the ninth birthday, the child *does not:*

- Exhibit a good appetite and continued weight gain (some children, especially girls, may already begin to show early signs of an eating disorder).

- Experience fewer illnesses.

- Show improved motor skills, in terms of agility, speed, and balance.

- Understand abstract concepts and use complex thought processes to problem-solve.

- Enjoy school and the challenge of learning.

- Follow through on multiple-step instructions.

- Express ideas clearly and fluently.

- Form friendships with other children and enjoy participating in group activities.

ELEVEN- TO THIRTEEN-YEAR-OLDS

- Parental influence is decreasing and some rebellion may occur

- Peer group is important and sets standards for behavior

- Worry about what others think

- Choose friends based on common interests
- Gender differences in interests
- Develop awareness and interest in opposite gender
- Begin to question adult authority
- Often reluctant to attend child care; are bored or think they can care for themselves
- May be moody and experience stress over physical changes of puberty
- May be rebellious as they seek their own identity
- Can think abstractly and apply logic to solving problems
- Have a good command of spoken and written language
- Girls develop gender characteristics, boys begin a growth spurt
- Early maturing is related to a positive self-image

Able to master physical skills necessary for playing games

Child's name _____   Age _____

Observer _____   Date _____

Developmental Checklist (by ten and eleven years)

Does the child . . .	Yes	No	Sometimes
Continue to increase in height and weight?	☐	☐	☐
Exhibit improving coordination: running, climbing, riding a bike, writing?	☐	☐	☐
Handle stressful situations without becoming overly upset or violent?	☐	☐	☐
Construct sentences using reasonably correct grammar: nouns, adverbs, verbs, adjectives?	☐	☐	☐
Understand concepts of time, distance, space, volume?	☐	☐	☐
Have one or two "best friends"?	☐	☐	☐
Maintain friendships over time?	☐	☐	☐
Approach challenges with a reasonable degree of self-confidence?	☐	☐	☐
Play cooperatively and follow group instructions?	☐	☐	☐
Begin to show an understanding of moral standards: right from wrong, fairness, honesty, good from bad?	☐	☐	☐
Look forward to, and enjoy, school?	☐	☐	☐
Appear to hear well and listen attentively?	☐	☐	☐

	Yes	No	Sometimes
Enjoy reasonably good health, with few episodes of illness or health-related complaints?	☐	☐	☐
Have a good appetite and enjoy mealtimes?	☐	☐	☐
Take care of own personal hygiene without assistance?	☐	☐	☐
Sleep through the night, waking up refreshed and energetic?	☐	☐	☐

DEVELOPMENTAL ALERTS

Check with a health care provider or early childhood specialist if, by the eleventh birthday, the child *does not:*

- Continue to grow at a rate appropriate for the child's gender.
- Show continued improvement of fine motor skills.
- Make or keep friends.
- Enjoy going to school and show interest in learning (have children's hearing and vision tested; vision and hearing problems affect children's ability to learn and their interest in learning).
- Approach new situations with reasonable confidence.
- Handle failure and frustration in a constructive manner.
- Sleep through the night or experiences prolonged problems with bedwetting, nightmares, or sleepwalking.

Child's name _____ Age _____
Observer _____ Date _____

Developmental Checklist (by twelve and thirteen years)

Does the child . . .	Yes	No	Sometimes
Appear to be growing: increasing height and maintaining a healthy weight (not too thin or too heavy)?	☐	☐	☐
Understand changes associated with puberty or have an opportunity to learn and ask questions?	☐	☐	☐
Complain of headaches or blurred vision?	☐	☐	☐
Have an abnormal posture or curving of the spine?	☐	☐	☐
Seem energetic and not chronically fatigued?	☐	☐	☐
Stay focused on a task and complete assignments?	☐	☐	☐

Remember and carry out complex instructions?	☐	☐	☐
Sequence, order, and classify objects?	☐	☐	☐
Use longer and more complex sentence structure?	☐	☐	☐
Engage in conversation; tell jokes and riddles?	☐	☐	☐
Enjoy playing organized games and team sports?	☐	☐	☐
Respond to anger-invoking situations without resorting to violence or physical aggression?	☐	☐	☐
Begin to understand and solve complex mathematical problems?	☐	☐	☐
Accept blame for actions on most occasions?	☐	☐	☐
Enjoy competition?	☐	☐	☐
Accept and carry out responsibility in a dependable manner?	☐	☐	☐
Go to bed willingly and wake up refreshed?	☐	☐	☐
Take pride in appearance; keep self reasonably clean?	☐	☐	☐

DEVELOPMENTAL ALERTS

Check with a health care provider or early childhood specialist if, by the thirteenth birthday, the child *does not:*

- Have movements that are smooth and coordinated.

- Have energy sufficient for playing, riding bikes, or engaging in other desired activities.

- Stay focused on tasks at hand.

- Understand basic cause-and-effect relationships.

- Handle criticism and frustration with a reasonable response (physical aggression and excessive crying could be an indication of other, underlying problems).

- Exhibit a healthy appetite (frequent skipping of meals is not typical for this age group).

- Make and keep friends.

(Some content in this section adapted from Allen, K. E., & Marotz, L. R. (2003). *Developmental Profiles: Pre-Birth through Twelve* (4th ed.), published by Thomson Delmar Learning.)

DEVELOPMENTAL MILESTONES BY SKILL

As with the list of milestones by age, this list is not exhaustive, but it can be used to arrange an environment or to plan activities in your room.

BIRTH TO ONE MONTH

Physical	Date Observed
Engages in primarily reflexive motor activity	
Maintains "fetal" position especially when sleeping	
Holds hands in a fist; does not reach for objects	
In prone position, head falls lower than the body's horizontal line with hips flexed and arms and legs hanging down	
Has good upper body muscle tone when supported under the arms	
Cognitive	
Blinks in response to fast-approaching object	
Follows a slowly moving object through a complete 180-degree arc	
Follows objects moved vertically if close to infant's face	
Continues looking about, even in the dark	
Begins to study own hand when lying in tonic neck reflex position	
Prefers to listen to mother's voice rather than a stranger's	
Language	
Cries and fusses as major forms of communication	
Reacts to loud noises by blinking, moving (or stopping), shifting eyes, making a startle response	
Shows preference for certain sounds (music and human voices) by calming down or quieting	

Language, continued	Date Observed
Turns head to locate voices and other sounds	
Makes occasional sounds other than crying	
Social/Emotional	
Experiences a short period of alertness immediately following birth	
Sleeps 17–19 hours a day; is gradually awake and responsive for longer periods	
Likes to be held close and cuddled when awake	
Shows qualities of individuality in responding or not responding to similar situations	
Begins to establish emotional attachment or bonding with parents and caregivers	
Begins to develop a sense of security/trust with parents and caregivers; responses to different individuals vary	

ONE TO FOUR MONTHS

Physical	Date Observed
Rooting and sucking reflexes are well developed	
In prone position, Landau reflex appears and baby raises head and upper body on arms	
Grasps with entire hand; strength insufficient to hold items	
Movements tend to be large and jerky	
Turns head side to side when in a supine (face up) position	
Begins rolling from front to back by turning head to one side and allowing trunk to follow	
Cognitive	
Fixes on a moving object held at 12 inches (30.5 cm)	
Continues to gaze in direction of moving objects that have disappeared	
Exhibits some sense of size/color/shape recognition of objects in the immediate environment	
Alternates looking at an object, at one or both hands, and then back at the object	
Moves eyes from one object to another.	
Focuses on small object and reaches for it; usually follows own hand movements	
Language	
Reacts to sounds (voice, rattle, doorbell); later will search for source by turning head	
Coordinates vocalizing, looking, and body movements in face-to-face exchanges with parent or caregiver	

Language, continued	Date Observed
Babbles or coos when spoken to or smiled at	
Imitates own sounds and vowel sounds produced by others	
Laughs out loud	
Social/Emotional	
Imitates, maintains, terminates, and avoids interactions	
Reacts differently to variations in adult voices	
Enjoys being held and cuddled at times other than feeding and bedtime	
Coos, gurgles, and squeals when awake	
Smiles in response to a friendly face or voice	
Entertains self for brief periods by playing with fingers, hands, and toes	

FOUR TO EIGHT MONTHS

Physical	Date Observed
Parachute reflex appears toward the end of this stage; swallowing reflex appears	
Uses finger and thumb (pincer grip) to pick up objects	
Reaches for objects with both arms simultaneously; later reaches with one hand	
Transfers objects from one hand to the other; grasps object using palmar grasp	
Handles, shakes, and pounds objects; puts everything in mouth	
Sits alone without support (holds head erect, back straight, arms propped forward for support)	
Cognitive	
Turns toward and locates familiar voices and sounds	
Uses hand, mouth, and eyes in coordination to explore own body, toys, and surroundings	
Imitates actions, such as pat-a-cake, waving bye-bye, and playing peek-a-boo	
Shows fear of falling from high places, such as changing table, stairs	
Looks over side of crib or high chair for objects dropped; delights in repeatedly throwing objects overboard for adult to retrieve	
Bangs objects together playfully; bangs spoon or toy on table	
Language	
Responds appropriately to own name and simple requests, such as "eat," "wave bye-bye"	
Imitates some nonspeech sounds, such as cough, tongue click, lip smacking	
Produces a full range of vowels and some consonants: r, s, z, th, and w	
Responds to variations in the tone of voice of others	

Language, continued	Date Observed
Expresses emotions (pleasure, satisfaction, anger) by making different sounds	
Babbles by repeating same syllable in a series: ba, ba, ba	
Social/Emotional	
Delights in observing surroundings; continuously watches people and activities	
Begins to develop an awareness of self as a separate individual from others	
Becomes more outgoing and social in nature: smiles, coos, reaches out	
Distinguishes among, and responds differently, to strangers, teachers, parents, siblings	
Responds differently and appropriately to facial expressions: frowns, smiles	
Imitates facial expressions, actions, and sounds	

EIGHT TO TWELVE MONTHS

Physical	Date Observed
Reaches with one hand leading to grasp an offered object or toy	
Manipulates objects, transferring them from one hand to the other	
Explores new objects by poking with one finger	
Uses deliberate pincer grip to pick up small objects, toys, and finger foods	
Stacks objects; also places objects inside one another	
Releases objects by dropping or throwing; cannot intentionally put an object down	
Begins pulling self to a standing position; begins to stand alone	
Cognitive	
Watches people, objects, and activities in the immediate environment	
Shows awareness of distant objects (15 to 20 feet away) by pointing at them	
Reaches for toys that are visible but out of reach	
Continues to drop first item when other toys or items are offered	
Recognizes the reversal of an object: cup upside down is still a cup	
Imitates activities: hitting two blocks together, playing pat-a-cake	
Language	
Babbles or jabbers to initiate social interaction; may shout to attract attention	
Shakes head for "no" and may nod for "yes"	
Responds by looking for voice when name is called	
Babbles in sentence-like sequences; followed by jargon (syllables/sounds with language-like inflection)	

Language, continued	Date Observed
Waves "bye-bye"; claps hands when asked	
Says "da-da" and "ma-ma"	
Social/Emotional	
Exhibits a definite fear of strangers; clings to, or hides behind, parent or caregiver ("stranger anxiety"); resists separating from familiar adult ("separation anxiety")	
Enjoys being near, and included in, daily activities of family members and teachers; is becoming more sociable and outgoing	
Enjoys novel experiences and opportunities to examine new objects	
Shows need to be picked up and held by extending arms upward, crying, or clinging to adult's legs	
Begins to exhibit assertiveness by resisting caregiver's requests; may kick, scream, or throw self on the floor	

ONE-YEAR-OLD

Physical	Date Observed
Crawls skillfully and quickly; gets to feet unaided	
Stands alone with feet spread apart, legs stiffened, and arms extended for support	
Walks unassisted near the end of this period (most children); falls often; not always able to maneuver around furniture or toys	
Uses furniture to lower self to floor; collapses backward into a sitting position or falls forward on hands and then sits	
Releases an object voluntarily	
Enjoys pushing or pulling toys while walking	
Cognitive	
Enjoys object-hiding activities: early on, will search same location for a hidden object; later will search in several locations	
Passes toy to other hand when offered a second object ("crossing the midline")	
Manages three to four objects by setting an object aside (on lap or floor) when presented with a new toy	
Puts toys in mouth less often	
Enjoys looking at picture books	
Demonstrates understanding of functional relationships (objects that belong together)	
Language	
Produces considerable "jargon": combines words/sounds into speech-like patterns	
Uses one word to convey an entire thought (holophrastic speech); later, produces two-word phrases to express a complete thought (telegraphic speech)	

Language, continued	Date Observed
Follows simple directions: "Give Daddy the cup"	
Points to familiar persons, animals, and toys when asked	
Identifies three body parts if someone names them: "Show me your nose (toe, ear)"	
Indicates a few desired objects/activities by name: "bye-bye," "cookie"; verbal request is often accompanied by an insistent gesture	
Social/Emotional	
Remains friendly toward others; usually less wary of strangers	
Helps pick up and put away toys	
Plays alone for short periods and does not play cooperatively	
Enjoys being held and read to	
Imitates adult actions in play	
Enjoys adult attention; likes to know that an adult is near; gives hugs and kisses	

TWO-YEAR-OLD

Physical	Date Observed
Walks with a more erect, heel-to-toe pattern; can maneuver around obstacles in pathway	
Runs with greater confidence; has fewer falls	
Squats for long periods while playing	
Climbs stairs unassisted (but not with alternating feet)	
Balances on one foot (for a few moments), jumps up and down, but may fall	
Begins to achieve toilet training (depending on physical and neurological development) although accidents should still be expected; will indicate readiness for toilet training	
Cognitive	
Exhibits better coordinated eye–hand movements; can put objects together, take them apart; fit large pegs into pegboard	
Begins to use objects for purposes other than intended (pushes block around as boat)	
Completes classification based on one dimension (separates toy dinosaurs from toy cars)	
Stares for long moments; seems fascinated by, or engrossed in, figuring out a situation	
Attends to self-selected activities for longer periods of time	
Shows discovery of cause and effect: squeezing the cat makes her scratch	

Language	Date Observed
Enjoys being read to if allowed to point, make relevant noises, turn pages	
Realizes that language is effective for getting others to respond to needs and preferences	
Uses 50 to 300 different words; vocabulary continuously increasing	
Has broken linguistic code; in other words, much of a two-year-old's talk has meaning to him or her	
Understands more language than can communicate verbally; most two-year-olds' receptive language is more developed than their expressive language	
Utters three- and four-word statements; uses conventional word order to form more complete sentences	
Social/Emotional	
Shows empathy and caring	
Continues to use physical aggression if frustrated or angry (more exaggerated in some children); physical aggression lessens as verbal skills improve	
Expresses frustration through temper tantrums; tantrum frequency peaks during this year; cannot be reasoned with while tantrum is in progress	
Finds it difficult to wait or take turns; often impatient	
Enjoys "helping" with household chores; imitates everyday activities	
Orders parents and teachers around; makes demands and expects immediate compliance	

THREE-YEAR-OLD

Physical	Date Observed
Walks up and down stairs unassisted using alternating feet; may jump from bottom step, landing on both feet	
Balances momentarily on one foot	
Kicks a large ball, catches a large bounced ball with both arms extended	
Feeds self; needs minimal assistance	
Jumps in place	
Pedals a small tricycle or Bigwheel	
Cognitive	
Listens attentively and makes relevant comments during age-appropriate stories, especially those related to home and family events	
Likes to look at books and may pretend to "read" to others or explain pictures	
Enjoys stories with riddles, guessing, and suspense	
Points with fair accuracy to correct pictures when given sound-alike words: keys–cheese; fish–dish; mouse–mouth	

Cognitive, continued	Date Observed
Plays realistically: feeds doll; hooks truck and trailer together	
Places eight to ten pegs in pegboard, or six round and six square blocks in formboard	
Language	
Talks about objects, events, and people not present: "Jerry has a pool in his yard"	
Talks about the actions of others: "Daddy's mowing the grass"	
Adds information to what has just been said: "Yeah, and then he grabbed it back"	
Answers simple questions appropriately	
Asks increasing numbers of questions, including location/identity of objects and people	
Uses increased speech forms to keep conversation going: "What did he do next?" "How come she hid?"	
Social/Emotional	
Seems to understand taking turns, but not always willing to do so	
Laughs frequently; is friendly and eager to please	
Has occasional nightmares and fears the dark, monsters, or fire	
Joins in simple games and group activities, sometimes hesitantly	
Talks to self often	
Uses objects symbolically in play: block of wood may be a truck, a ramp, a bat	

FOUR-YEAR-OLD

Physical	Date Observed
Walks a straight line (tape or chalkline on the floor)	
Hops on one foot	✓
Pedals and steers a wheeled toy with confidence; avoids obstacles and oncoming "traffic"	✓
Climbs ladders, trees, playground equipment	✓
Jumps over objects 5 or 6 inches (12.5 to 15 cm) high; lands with both feet together	✓
Runs, starts, stops, and moves around obstacles with ease	✓
Cognitive	
Stacks at least five graduated cubes largest to smallest; builds a pyramid of six blocks	✓
Indicates if paired words sound the same or different: sheet–feet, ball–wall	✓

Cognitive, continued	Date Observed
Names 18–20 uppercase letters near the end of this year; may be able to print several and write own name; may recognize some printed words (especially those that have special meaning)	
Some begin to read simple books (alphabet books with few words per page and many pictures)	
Likes stories about how things grow and operate	
Delights in wordplay, creating silly language	✓
Language	
Uses the prepositions "on," "in," and "under"	✓
Uses possessives consistently: "hers," "theirs," "baby's"	
Answers "Whose?" "Who?" "Why?" and "How many?"	
Produces elaborate sentence structures	✓
Uses almost entirely intelligible speech	✓
Begins to correctly use the past tense of verbs: "Mommy closed the door," "Daddy went to work."	✓
Social/Emotional	
Is outgoing and friendly; overly enthusiastic at times	✓
Changes moods rapidly and unpredictably; often throws tantrum over minor frustrations; sulks over being left out	
Holds conversations and shares strong emotions with imaginary playmates or companions; invisible friends are common	
Boasts, exaggerates, and "bends" the truth with made-up stories or claims; tests limits with "bathroom" talk	
Cooperates with others; participates in group activities	✓
Shows pride in accomplishments; seeks frequent adult approval	✓

FIVE-YEAR-OLD

Physical	Date Observed
Walks backward, heel to toe	
Walks unassisted up and down stairs, alternating feet	
Learns to turn somersaults (should be taught the right way in order to avoid injury)	
Touches toes without flexing knees	
Catches a ball thrown from 3 feet away	
Rides a tricycle or wheeled toy with speed and skillful steering; some learn to ride bicycles, usually with training wheels	✓

Cognitive	Date Observed
Forms rectangle from two triangular cuts	✓
Builds steps with set of small blocks	✓
Understands concept of same shape, same size	'
Sorts objects on the basis of two dimensions, such as color and form	✓
Sorts objects so that all things in the group have a single common feature	
Understands smallest and shortest; places objects in order from shortest to tallest, smallest to largest	✓
Language	
Has vocabulary of 1,500 words or more	
Tells a familiar story while looking at pictures in a book	
Uses functional definitions: a ball is to bounce; a bed is to sleep in	
Identifies and names four to eight colors	
Recognizes the humor in simple jokes; makes up jokes and riddles	
Produces sentences with five to seven words; much longer sentences are not unusual	✓
Social/Emotional	
Enjoys friendships; often has one or two special playmates	✓
Shares toys, takes turns, plays cooperatively (with occasional lapses); is often quite generous	✓
Participates in play and activities with other children; suggests imaginative and elaborate play ideas	
Is affectionate and caring, especially toward younger or injured children and animals	✓
Follows directions and carries out assignments usually; generally does what parent or teacher requests	✓
Continues to need adult comfort and reassurance, but may be less open in seeking and accepting comfort	

SIX-YEAR-OLD

Physical	Date Observed
Has increased muscle strength; typically boys are stronger than girls of similar size	
Gains greater control over large and fine motor skills; movements are more precise and deliberate although some clumsiness persists	
Enjoys vigorous physical activity: running, jumping, climbing, and throwing	
Moves constantly, even when trying to sit still	

Physical, continued	Date Observed
Has increased dexterity, eye–hand coordination, and improved motor functioning, which facilitate learning to ride a bicycle, swim, swing a bat, or kick a ball	
Enjoys art projects: likes to paint, model with clay, "make things," draw and color, work with wood	
Cognitive	
Shows increased attention; works at tasks for longer periods, although concentrated effort is not always consistent	
Understands simple time markers (today, tomorrow, yesterday) or uncomplicated concepts of motion (cars go faster than bicycles)	
Recognizes seasons and major holidays and the activities associated with each	
Enjoys puzzles, counting and sorting activities, paper-and-pencil mazes, and games that involve matching letters and words with pictures	
Recognizes some words by sight; attempts to sound out words (some may read well by this time)	
Identifies familiar coins: pennies, nickels, dimes, quarters	
Language	
Loves to talk, often nonstop; may be described as a chatterbox	
Carries on adult-like conversations; asks many questions	
Learns five to ten new words daily; vocabulary consists of 10,000 to 14,000 words	
Uses appropriate verb tenses, word order, and sentence structure	
Uses language (not tantrums or physical aggression) to express displeasure: "That's mine! Give it back, you dummy."	
Talks self through steps required in simple problem-solving situations (although the "logic" may be unclear to adults)	
Social/Emotional	
Experiences mood swings: "best friends" then "worst enemies"; loving then uncooperative and irritable; especially unpredictable toward mother or primary caregiver	
Becomes less dependent on parents as friendship circle expands; still needs closeness and nurturing but has urges to break away and "grow up"	
Needs and seeks adult approval, reassurance, and praise; may complain excessively about minor hurts to gain more attention	
Continues to be egocentric; still sees events almost entirely from own perspective: views everything and everyone as there for child's own benefit	
Easily disappointed and frustrated by self-perceived failure	
Has difficulty composing and soothing self; cannot tolerate being corrected or losing at games; may sulk, cry, refuse to play, or reinvent rules to suit own purposes	

SEVEN-YEAR-OLD

Physical	Date Observed
Exhibits large and fine motor control that is more finely tuned:	
Tends to be cautious in undertaking more challenging physical activities, such as climbing up or jumping down from high places	
Practices a new motor skill repeatedly until mastered then moves on to something else	
Finds floor more comfortable than furniture when reading or watching television; legs often in constant motion	
Uses knife and fork appropriately, but inconsistently	
Tightly grasps pencil near the tip; rests head on forearm, lowers head almost to the table top when doing pencil-and-paper tasks	
Cognitive	
Understands concepts of space and time in both logical and practical ways: a year is "a long time"; 100 miles is "far away"	
Begins to grasp Piaget's concepts of conservation (the shape of a container does not necessarily reflect what it can hold)	
Gains a better understanding of cause and effect: "If I'm late for school again, I'll be in big trouble."	
Tells time by the clock and understands calendar time—days, months, years, seasons	
Plans ahead: "I'm saving this cookie for tonight."	
Shows marked fascination with magic tricks; enjoys putting on "shows" for parents and friends	
Language	
Enjoys storytelling; likes to write short stories, tell imaginative tales	
Uses adult-like sentence structure and language in conversation; patterns reflect cultural and geographical differences	
Becomes more precise and elaborate in use of language; greater use of descriptive adjectives and adverbs	
Uses gestures to illustrate conversations	
Criticizes own performance: "I didn't draw that right," "Her picture is better than mine."	
Verbal exaggeration commonplace: "I ate ten hot dogs at the picnic."	
Social/Emotional	
Is cooperative and affectionate toward adults and less frequently annoyed with them; sees humor in everyday happenings	
Likes to be the "teacher's helper"; eager for teacher's attention and approval but less obvious about seeking it	

Social/Emotional, continued	Date Observed
Seeks out friendships; friends are important, but can stay busy if no one is available	
Quarrels less often, although squabbles and tattling continue in both one-on-one and group play	
Complains that family decisions are unjust, that a particular sibling gets to do more or is given more	
Blames others for own mistakes; makes up alibis for personal shortcomings: " I could have made a better one, but my teacher didn't give me enough time."	

EIGHT-YEAR-OLD

Physical	Date Observed
Enjoys vigorous activity; likes to dance, roller blade, swim, wrestle, bicycle, fly kites	
Seeks opportunities to participate in team activities and games: soccer, baseball, kickball	
Exhibits significant improvement in agility, balance, speed, and strength	
Copies words and numbers from blackboard with increasing speed and accuracy; has good eye–hand coordination	
Possesses seemingly endless energy	
Cognitive	
Collects objects; organizes and displays items according to more complex systems; bargains and trades with friends to obtain additional pieces	
Saves money for small purchases; eagerly develops plans to earn cash for odd jobs; studies catalogues and magazines for items to purchase	
Begins taking an interest in what others think and do; understands there are differences of opinion, cultures, distant countries	
Accepts challenge and responsibility with enthusiasm; delights in being asked to perform tasks at home and in school; interested in being rewarded	
Likes to read and work independently; spends considerable time planning and making lists	
Understands perspective (shadow, distance, shape); drawings reflect more realistic portrayal of objects	
Language	
Delights in telling jokes and riddles	
Understands and carries out multiple-step instructions (up to five steps); may need directions repeated because of not listening to the entire request	
Enjoys writing letters or sending e-mail messages to friends; includes imaginative and detailed descriptions	

Language, continued	Date Observed
Uses language to criticize and compliment others; repeats slang and curse words	
Understands and follows rules of grammar in conversation and written form	
Is intrigued with learning secret word codes and using code language	
Converses fluently with adults; can think and talk about past and future: "What time are we leaving to get to the swim meet next week?"	
Social/Emotional	
Begins forming opinions about moral values and attitudes; declares things right or wrong	
Plays with two or three "best" friends, most often the same age and gender; also enjoys spending some time alone	
Seems less critical of own performance but is easily frustrated when unable to complete a task or when the product does not meet expectations	
Enjoys team games and activities; values group membership and acceptance by peers	
Continues to blame others or makes up alibis to explain own shortcomings or mistakes	
Enjoys talking on the telephone with friends	

Some content in this section is adapted from Allen, K. E., & Marotz, L. R. (2003). *Developmental Profiles: Pre-Birth through Twelve* (4th ed.), published by Thomson Delmar Learning.

PLAY MATERIALS FOR CHILDREN

Children construct their own understanding of the world around them as they interact with appropriate materials and with other people. Teachers play an important role in providing choices of good quality playthings that match children's developmental abilities and interests. When budgets are limited, it is vital for teachers to be able to select toys and materials that will provide optimum learning opportunities. Creative teachers learn how to "scrounge" for toys, and to make playthings out of recycled materials.

CRITERIA FOR SELECTING PLAY EQUIPMENT FOR YOUNG CHILDREN

A young child's playthings should be as free of detail as possible.

- Too much detail hampers a child's freedom to express himself.

- "Unstructured" toys, which allow the imagination free rein, include blocks, construction sets, clay, sand, and paints.

A good plaything should stimulate children to do things for themselves.

- Equipment that makes the child a spectator, may entertain but has little or no play value.

- Play equipment should encourage children to explore and create or offer dramatic play potential.

Young children need large, easily manipulated playthings.

- Toys too small can be frustrating because the child's undeveloped muscular coordination cannot handle smaller forms and shapes.

- A child's muscles develop through play, so equipment should allow for climbing and balancing.

The material of which a plaything is constructed has an important role in the play of the young child.

- Warmth and pleasurable touch are significant (wood and cloth have been established as the most satisfactory materials).

- The plaything's durability is of utmost importance.

- Play materials must be sturdy; axles and wheels must be able to support a child's weight.

- Children hate to see their toys break.

- Some materials break readily, proving them to be expensive.

The toy must "work."

- Be sure parts move correctly and that maintenance will be easy.

A plaything's construction should be simple enough for a child to comprehend.

- This strengthens his understanding and experience of the world around him.

- Mechanics should be visible and easily grasped; small children will take them apart to see how they tick.

A plaything should encourage cooperative play.

- Provide an environment that stimulates children to work and play together.

The total usefulness of the plaything must be considered in comparing price.

- Will it last several children through several stages of their playing lives?

The lists that follow suggest the materials that are priorities for children at particular levels of development.

FOR YOUNG INFANTS (BIRTH THROUGH 6 MONTHS)

- unbreakable mirrors that can be attached low on walls, or near changing tables and cribs

- mobiles and visuals hung out of reach

- grasping toys: simple rattles, squeeze toys, keys on ring, clutch or texture balls

- hanging toys for batting

- wrist or ankle bells

FOR OLDER, MOBILE INFANTS (7 THROUGH 12 MONTHS)

- soft rubber animals for grasping

- simple one-piece vehicles 6–8 inches, with large wheels

- grasping toys for skill development: toys on suction cups, stacking rings, nesting cups, squeeze toys, plastic pop beads, bean bags, busy boxes

- containers and objects to fill and dump

- small cloth, plastic, and board books

- soft cloth or foam blocks for stacking

- simple floating objects for water play

- balls of all kinds, including some with special effects

- large unbreakable mirrors

FOR TODDLERS (1 THROUGH 3 YEARS)

For Fine Motor Skills

- nesting materials

- sand and water play toys: funnels, colanders, small sand tools

- simple activity boxes, with doors, lids, switches, more complex after about 18 months: turning knob or key

- pegboards with large pegs

- four- to five-piece piece stacking materials

- pop beads and stringing beads

- simple three- to five-piece piece puzzles, with knobs, familiar shapes

- simple matching materials

- books, including tactile books, cloth, plastic, and board picture books

For Gross Motor Skills

- push and pull toys

- stable riding toys with four wheels and no pedals

- balls of all sizes

- tunnels for crawling through

For Pretend Play

- small wood or plastic people and animal figures

- small cars and trucks

- plastic dishes and pots and pans

- telephones

For Sensory Play

- play dough

- fingerpaint

- large nontoxic crayons

- sturdy paper

- simple musical instruments

FOR CHILDREN (3 THROUGH 5 YEARS)

For Gross Motor Play

- small wagons and wheelbarrows

- replications of adult tools for pushing and pretend play, such as lawn mower, shopping cart

- scooters

- tricycles and other vehicles with steering ability

- riding toys for more than one child

- balls of all sizes, especially 10–12 inch balls for kicking and throwing

- hollow plastic bat and lightweight ball

- slides and ladders

- outdoor building materials, tires, and other loose parts

For Exploration and Mastery Play

- sand and water play: measures, funnels, tubes, sand tools

- construction materials: unit blocks, large hollow blocks

- Lego®-type plastic interlocking blocks

- puzzles, including fit-in puzzles and large, simple jigsaw puzzles, with varying numbers of pieces, according to children's age

- pattern-making materials: beads for stringing, pegboards, mosaic boards, feltboards, color cubes

- dressing, lacing, and stringing: sewing cards and dressing frames

- collections of small plastic objects for matching, sorting, and ordering, by color, shape, size, or other category concepts

- simple, concrete number materials for counting and matching to numerals

- measuring materials: scales, measuring cups for liquids

- science materials: magnifying glass, color paddles, objects from the natural world, including pets

- beginning computer programs

- games: dominoes, lotto games, bingo by color, number, or picture, first board games that use concepts such as color or counting, memory

- books of all kinds: picture books, realistic stories, alphabet picture books, poetry, information books

- writing center materials: clipboards, colored pencils, old calendars, envelopes, notepads, stationery, rubber stamps and ink pads, rulers, magnetic letters, stencil shapes, stickers, file cards, and office materials

For Pretend Play

- housekeeping equipment

- variety of dress-ups, including those related to various roles and themes

- transportation toys

- animal and human figures for play scenes

- full-length, unbreakable mirror

For Creative Play

- art and craft materials: crayons, markers, easel, paintbrushes, paint and fingerpaint, varieties of paper, chalkboard and chalk, safety scissors, glue, collage materials, clay and play dough, and tools to use with them

- workbench with hammer, saw, and nails

- musical instruments

- recorded music for singing, movement and dancing, listening, and for using with rhythm instruments

FOR CHILDREN (6 THROUGH 8 YEARS)

For Gross Motor Play

- balls and sports equipment for beginning team play, such as soccer, baseball

- complex climbing structures: ropes, ladders, rings, hanging bars

- materials for target practice

- mats for acrobatics

- bicycles and scooters

For Exploration and Mastery Play

- construction materials for large constructions and for creating models, including metal parts and nuts and bolts

- puzzles: 100-piece jigsaw puzzles, three-dimensional puzzles like Rubik's cubes

- craft materials for braiding, weaving, knitting, leather craft, jewelry making, sewing

- pattern-making materials: mosaic tiles, geometric puzzles

- games: word games, simple card games, reading and spelling games, number and counting games, beginning strategy games such as checkers

- materials for specific learning: printing materials, math manipulatives, measuring materials, science materials, and computer programs for language arts, number and concept development, and for problem-solving activities

- books at a variety of levels for beginning readers—see the Resources list in this supplement

For Creative Activities

- variety of markers, colored pencils, chalks, paintbrushes and paints, art papers for tracing and drawing

- clay and tools, including pottery wheel

- workbench with wood and variety of tools

- real instruments such as guitars and recorders

- music for singing and movement

- audiovisual materials for independent use

Some ideas adapted from Bronson, M. (1995). *The Right Stuff for Children Birth to 8: Selecting Play Materials to Support Development.* Washington, DC: NAEYC.

Remember that recycled materials and other loose parts have many uses for exploration and creativity. These materials can be valuable tools in a number of curriculum areas:

- Empty plastic containers—detergent bottles, bleach bottles, old refrigerator containers, which can be used for constructing scoops, storing art materials, etc.

- Buttons—all colors and sizes, which are excellent for collages, assemblages, as well as sorting, counting, matching, etc.

- Eggshells, which can be washed, dried, and colored with food coloring for art projects

- Coffee or shortening cans and lids, which can be covered with adhesive paper and used for storage of art supplies, games, and manipulatives materials

- Magazines with colorful pictures, which are excellent for making collages, murals, and posters

- Scraps of fabric—felt, silk, cotton, oil cloth, etc., which can be used to make "fabric boards" with the name of each fabric written under a small swatch attached to the board, as well as for collages, puppets, etc.

- Yarn scraps, which can be used for separating buttons into sets; also for art activities

- Styrofoam™ scraps

- Scraps of lace, rickrack, or decorative trim

- Bottles with sprinkler tops, which are excellent for water play and for mixing water as children fingerpaint

- Wallpaper books of discontinued patterns

- Paper doilies

- Discarded wrapping paper

- Paint color cards from paint/hardware stores

- Old paintbrushes

- Old jewelry and beads

- Old muffin tins, which are effective for sorting small objects and mixing paint

- Tongue depressors or ice cream sticks, which can be used as counters for math, and are good for art construction projects, stick puppets, etc.

- Wooden clothespins, which can be used for making "people," for construction projects, for hanging up paintings to dry

Adapted from Mayesky, M. (2006). *Creative Activities for Young Children* (8th ed.), published by Thomson Delmar Learning.

If you are responsible for ordering supplies for your classroom or early childhood program, the following guidelines will be useful.

BASIC PROGRAM EQUIPMENT AND MATERIALS FOR AN EARLY CHILDHOOD CENTER

Indoor Equipment

The early childhood room should be arranged into well-planned areas of interest, such as the housekeeping and doll corner, block building, and others, to encourage children to play in small groups throughout the playroom, engaging in activities of their special interest, rather than attempting to play in one large group.

The early childhood center must provide selections of indoor play equipment from many areas of interest. Selection should be of sufficient quantities so that children can participate in a wide range of activities. Many pieces of equipment can be homemade. Consider the age and developmental levels of the children when making selections.

Playroom Furnishings

- Tables—seat four to six children (18" high for three-year-olds, 20"–22" high for four- and five-year-olds)
- Chairs—10" high for three-year-olds, 12"–14" high for four- and five-year-olds
- Open shelves—26" high, 12" deep, 12" between shelves
- Lockers—12" wide, 12" deep, 32"–36" high

Housekeeping or Doll Corner

Item	Number Recommended for 10 Children
Dolls	3
Doll clothes	Variety
Doll bed—should be large enough for a child to get into, bedding	1
Doll high chair	1
Small table, four chairs set	
Tea party dishes	6-piece set with tray
Stove—child size, approximately 24" high, 23" long, 12" wide	1
Sink—child size, approximately 24" high, 23" long, 12" wide	1
Refrigerator—child size, approximately 28" high, 23" long, 12" wide	1
Pots and pans, empty food cartons, measuring cups, spoons, etc.	Variety
Mop, broom, dustpan	1
Ironing board and iron	1
Clothespins and clothesline	1
Toy telephones	2
Dress-up box—men's and women's hats, neckties, pocketbooks, shoes, old dresses, scarves, jewelry, etc.	Variety
Mirror	1

Art Supplies

Item	Number Recommended for 10 Children
Newsprint paper 18" x 24"	1 ream
Colored paper—variety	3 packages
Large crayons	10 boxes
Tempera paint—red, yellow, blue, black, white	1 can each
Long-handled paintbrushes—making a stroke from 1/2" to 1" wide	10–12
Easels	1
Fingerpaint paper—glazed paper such as shelf, freezer, or butcher's paper	1 roll
Paste	1 quart
Blunt scissors	10
Collage—collection of bits of colored paper, cut-up gift wrappings, ribbons, cotton, string, scraps of fabric, etc., for pasting	Variety
Magazines for cutting and pasting	Variety

Item	Number Recommended for 10 Children
Clay—play dough, homemade dough clay	50 pounds
Cookie cutters, rolling pins	Variety
Smocks or aprons to protect children's clothes	10

Block Building Area

Item	Number Recommended for 10 Children
Unit blocks—purchased or homemade (directions are available)	276 pieces, 11 shapes
Large, lightweight blocks	Variety
Small wooden or rubber animals and people	Variety
Small trucks, airplanes, cars, and boats	12
Medium airplanes	3
Medium boats	2
Medium-sized trucks—12" to 24"	3

Music Corner

- record player, tape player, CD player
- suitable records, tapes, and CDs
- rhythm instruments
- dress-up scarves for dancing

Manipulative Toys

Item	Number Recommended for 10 Children
Wooden inlay puzzles—approximately 5 to 20 pieces	6
Color cone	1
Nested blocks	1 set
Pegboard—variety of shapes and sizes	1
Large spools and beads for stringing	2 sets
Toys that have parts that fit into one another	2
Lotto games	2
Dominoes	1 set

Books and Stories(20–30 books)

A carefully selected book collection for the various age levels should include the following:

- transportation, birds and animals, family life

- community helpers, science, nonsense rhymes

- Mother Goose rhymes, poems, and stories

- homemade picture books

- collection of pictures classified by subject

- library books to enrich the collection

Nature Study and Science

- aquarium or fishbowls

- plastic materials

- magnifying glass, prism, magnet, thermometers

- growing indoor plants, garden plot

- additional material such as stones, leaves, acorns, birds' nests, caterpillars, worms, tadpoles, etc.

Woodworking Center

Basic woodworking operations are

- sanding

- gluing

- hammering

- holding (with a vise or clamp)

- fastening (with screws)

- drilling

- sawing

Materials for a woodworking center include:

- sturdy workbench (or table)

- woodworking tools: broad-headed nails 3/4" to 1-1/2" long, C-clamp or vise (to hold wood), flat-headed hammer weighing about 12 ounces for beginning woodworking experiences, later a claw hammer may be added, 14-inch saw with 10 teeth to the inch

- soft white pine lumber scraps (it is difficult to drive nails into hardwood; plywood is not suitable either); packing boxes of soft pine can be disassembled and used for hammering work

Sand Play

- For outdoors, sand should be confined so it is not scattered over the rest of the playground.

- Outdoor area should be large enough for several children to move about without crowding each other.

- A 10- to 12-inch ledge around a sandbox can serve as a boundary and provide children with a working surface or a seat.

- Keep sand 6" to 8" below the top of the ledge so that it is less likely to spill out.

- Sand should be about 18" deep so that children can dig or make tunnels.

- Four or five inches of gravel on the bottom of the sandbox provides drainage.

- Basic equipment includes plastic or metal kitchen utensils— cups, spoons, pails, shovels, sifters, funnels, scoops, bowls.

Water Play

- This can be either an indoor or outdoor activity, depending on climate.

- Use clear plastic water basins on a stand with wheels to allow them to be moved to any area of a room.

- When using plastic basins, children can see through the sides and the bottom.

- For tables on a carpeted floor, use a plastic runner to protect the carpet.

- Materials include clear tubing, sponges, strainers, funnels, corks, pitchers, and measuring cups; for added interest use rotary beaters, spoons, small bowls, plastic basters, and straws.

Outdoor Equipment

Outdoor play equipment should be grouped according to use. For example, plan for both active and quiet play; allow for free areas for use of wheel toys. Suggested basic outdoor play equipment for the early childhood program includes:

- climbing structure(s)
- large and small packing boxes
- slide
- swings with canvas seats
- wagons and wheelbarrows
- pedal toys—tricycles, cars, etc.
- sandbox with spoons, shovels, pails, etc.
- balls
- a variety of salvage materials: rubber tires, tire tubes, lengths of garden hose, ropes, and cardboard boxes

Note: many activities, such as housekeeping play and art activities, at times can be transferred to the outdoor area.

Use this checklist to evaluate your playground setup:

_____ Pathways are clear and spacious enough between areas so that traffic flows well and equipment does not obstruct the children's movement.

_____ Space and equipment are organized so that children are readily visible and easily supervised by adults.

_____ Different activity areas are separated. (Tricycle paths are separate from swings, sandbox is separate from climbing area.)

_____ Open space is available for active play.

_____ There is some space for quiet play.

_____ Dramatic play can be set up outdoors, as space is available.

_____ Art activities can be set up outdoors.

_____ A portion of the play area is covered for use in wet weather.

_____ A storage area is available for play equipment.

_____ A drinking fountain is available.

_____ The area has readily accessible restrooms.

OBSERVATION AND ASSESSMENT

There are a variety of tools that can be used to assess children's development. Using assessment tools in conjunction with developmental milestones helps caregivers recognize a child's developmental accomplishments as well as determine the child's next growth steps. Not all children will give as much time to the teacher's directions. The teacher needs to observe each child to determine the level to which each child is performing independently so that instruction can begin. This knowledge is useful in planning curriculum, designing the room environment for success, and in establishing appropriate techniques that help children manage their own behavior. No doubt your college practicum experience taught you the logistics of observing: using objective descriptions and recording specific, dated, brief, and factual information. Observation can take many forms:

- Anecdotal records

- Running records

- Checklists

- Time or event sampling

ANECDOTAL RECORD

Anecdotal records are brief notes kept by the teacher while the child is performing a task. At first this may seem daunting, but it will become part of your everyday routine. Keep a small spiral notebook and pen or pencil in your pocket. When a child begins an activity, watch what the child does and write down three or four things that you actually observe the child doing. Remember the facts and only the facts. For example:

Jing Mae picked up magnifying glass—looked at flower—picked up paper—went to easel and began to draw a flower

As time permits, probably during nap time, the brief notes are turned into a full scenario so that anyone could read the record at a later date:

ANECDOTAL RECORD

Child's Name: Johnny H.
Observer's Name: Jorge

Age: 7 yr. 5 mo.
Date: April 27, 2005

What actually happened / What I saw	Developmental Interpretation (Select 1 or 2 of the following)	
Jing Mae picked up the magnifying glass set out for the children to pick up as they choose, looked closely at the flower. Brought the flower to her teacher who shared in the observation. A conversation took place. Jing Mae then went to the art area and drew a picture of a flower.	Interest in learning	
	Self-esteem/self-concept	X
	Cultural acceptance	
	Problem solving	
	Interest in real-life mathematical concepts	
	Interactions with adults	X
	Literacy	
	Interactions with peers	
	Language expression/comprehension	
	Self-regulation	
	Safe/healthy behavior	
	Self-help skills	
	Gross motor skills	
	Fine motor skills	X

ANECDOTAL RECORD

Child's Name: Date:
Observer's Name:

What actually happened/What I saw	Developmental Interpretation (Select 1 or 2 of the following)	
	Interest in learning	
	Self-esteem/self-concept	
	Cultural acceptance	
	Problem solving	
	Interest in real-life mathematical concepts	
	Interactions with adults	
	Literacy	
	Interactions with peers	
	Language expression/comprehension	
	Self-regulation	
	Safe/healthy behavior	
	Self-help skills	
	Gross motor skills	
	Fine motor skills	

RUNNING RECORD

Another form of authentic assessment is the **running record.** It covers a longer time span and gives more information than an anecdotal record. Often it may have a specific developmental focus such as "social interactions." A running record will give you information about other developmental areas because of its very detailed nature. This form of observation requires the caregiver to not be involved with children for several minutes while writing the observation. You will be setting yourself apart from the children and writing continuously, in as much detail as possible. You will write what the child does and says, by herself and in interactions with other people and materials. Use objective phrases and avoid interpretative and judgmental language. Note that the format for this form of assessment has two columns. The left column is for writing the actual observations and the right column is for connecting the observations to aspects of development. Remember to date all observations so you can notice developmental change over time.

RUNNING RECORD

Child's Name: Trish H.

Observer's Name: Jorge

Age: 7 yr. 5 mo.

Date: April 27, 2005

Developmental Focus: Social interactions with peers

Meaghan and Luke were playing in the water table. The teacher had left out objects and a chart for the children to predict which objects would sink and float. After making their predictions, the children began the experiment. Meaghan told Luke, "I am right, you are wrong. The cotton ball will float." Luke said, "Let's try it and see." The cotton ball was placed in the water. At first it floated, but after a few seconds, the cotton ball sank. The teacher came over to see how things were going and questioned Luke as to why the cotton ball sank. He said, "Because the cotton ball drank the water." Meaghan was not happy about being wrong, but conceded for now. The two moved on to the next object and their prediction.	Participates in cooperative activities Early literacy/expressive language Expresses empathy Communicates knowledge of growing skills Self-regulation/controls emotions Stands up for own rights Asks for what she needs Gross motor skills Math skill Self-awareness

CHECKLIST

A **checklist** is often used as a means of assessment because it is one of the easiest assessment tools to use. A checklist consists of a predetermined list of clearly observable developmental criteria for which the observer indicates "yes" or "no." The observer reads the developmental criteria and makes a checkmark if the decision is a "yes." This form of assessment requires that no additional notes be recorded. Many teachers design their own checklists to fit the specific needs of their program. The following checklist is an example of one that might be used to assess social skills of children.

Make checklists for each center in your classroom and hang them on clipboards. When you observe the children at play in each center, check off skills by placing a date in the appropriate box.

SOCIAL SKILLS CHECKLIST

Child's Name: Age: yr.   mo.
Observer's Name:

Skills	Dates
☐ Desires and can work near other children	
☐ Interacts with other children	
☐ Takes turns with other children	
☐ Enters play with others in positive manner	
☐ Shares materials and supplies	
☐ Stands up for own rights in positive manner	
☐ Forms friendships with peers	
☐ Engages in positive commentary on other children's work	
☐ Shows empathy	
☐ Negotiates compromises with other children	
☐ Demonstrates pro-social behavior	
☐ Participates in cooperative group activities	
☐ Resolves conflicts with adult prompts	
☐ Resolves conflicts without adult prompts	

TIME OR EVENT SAMPLING

The last type of observation that a teacher should perform is a time or event sampling. These are similar in focus, but different, too. A **time sampling** asks the teacher to set a timer and each time the timer goes off, the teacher looks at a particular child and writes down what the child is doing. Again only the facts are written:

The timer is set to go off every ten minutes. I will look at Johnny and see what he is doing when I hear the timer. The timer goes off, I look at Johnny. *He is sorting the objects by color.* The timer goes off again. *He now has three piles.*

As mentioned, an **event sampling** is similar, only the teacher looks at events instead of being directed by a timer. The teacher zeros in on an event and writes down all things that she sees pertaining to the event.

EVENT SAMPLE		
Antecedent	**Behavior**	**Consequence**
Johnny is sorting shapes.	He chooses to sort by color.	He does not talk while doing his work. The teacher is watching to see what he will do with the two shapes that have more than one color. Johnny puts those back in the box.

Assessment and observation may seem overwhelming as you begin your career in Early Childhood. Do not shy away from it. Take the challenge and begin to look for the positive aspects of learning and mastering a new skill. Picture yourself as a student in your classroom and imagine what it is like to perfect something your teacher has just asked you to do. How does it make you feel? Now begin.

CURRICULUM AND LESSON PLANS

- You have the day planned for outdoor activities and there is an unexpected rainstorm. What will you do?

- It is your day off and you get a call at the last minute to cover for a co-worker who is ill. You find out that nothing has been planned. What activities can you implement quickly?

- You were promised that the materials you needed for your planned art activity would be on site when you arrived at work, but there was a shipping delay and they aren't there. What is an alternative activity you can easily set up and implement?

Being prepared at all times with a few backup activities will make your job much less stressful. Some of the activities listed here require only a few materials that you might want to have on hand at all times.

MATH LESSON PLANS

One-to-one Correspondence
Developmental Focus: Cognitive

Goal: Children will demonstrate knowledge of the concept one-to-one by setting a table.

Age Range: 3–5

Materials: 4 plates, 4 cups, 4 forks, 4 spoons, 4 napkins, 4 placemats, table, chairs, snack

Procedure: Put one chair on each side of the table. Then place one placemat on the table by each chair. On the placemat, put the plate in the center. Continue adding the fork, spoon, napkin, and cup to each setting. Then serve a snack.

Sorting
Developmental Focus: Cognitive

Goal: Children will sort objects by two characteristics.

Age Range: 3–5

Materials: circles, squares, and triangles each in three different colors, plate that matches each color chosen, plate that has each shape drawn on it.

Procedure: Put the plates on the table. Place the pile of shapes in the middle. Ask the children to sort the shapes onto the plates (use the colored ones first). Once complete, remove two of the colors and put the shape plates on the table. Ask the children if the shapes can be sorted again using the new plates on the table.

Counting
Developmental Focus: Cognitive

Goal: Children will count up to five objects.

Age Range: 3–5

Materials: 5 objects that are connected by use (marker, pencil, paper, crayon, scissors)

Procedure: Place the objects on the table. Call a child over to the table. Count the objects on the table in front of the child. Then ask the child to count the objects with you. If this is successful, then ask the child to count them on their own.

Graphing
Developmental Focus: Cognitive

Goal: Children will graph their responses to the question, what is your favorite fruit?

Age Range: 3–5

Materials: fruit stickers (enough for each child to have one), paper, marker

Procedure: Take the paper and put it on the easel. Place one of each fruit sticker on the bottom of the paper to form columns. Use the marker to draw the base line and the column lines. Give each child a sticker that matches their favorite fruit. Ask them to place their sticker on the paper in the right column. Help if necessary. When everyone has had a turn, ask the children questions about the data collected on the graph. For example, how many children like peaches?

Lotto Game (Individual)
Developmental Focus: Cognitive

Goal: To allow child to individually explore concept of matching.

Age Range: 3 and 4 years old

Materials: lotto game on tray (example is matching pictures of sand toys)

Procedure: Make or purchase lotto game with game board and matching cards. Make a placemat for tray with outlines for board and cards. Child plays matching game, exploring concept. Facilitate child's free exploration of lotto game by limited interaction, as appropriate. Child replaces pieces on tray, returns to shelf.

Lotto Game (Small Group)
Developmental Focus: Cognitive, Social

Goal: Children will be allowed to participate in a group matching game.

Age Range: 3 and 4 years old

Materials: lotto game with four game boards and corresponding cards (example is matching pictures of pets)

Procedure: Make or purchase lotto game with game board and matching cards. Make a placemat for tray with outlines for board and cards. Invite children to play a matching game. Each child is given a game board. Describe a card, wait for child to find on the board. Children collect "matches" until board is filled.

What's Our Favorite Apple?
Developmental Focus: Cognitive

Goal: The children will have an opportunity to graph apple preferences.

Age Range: 3 and 4 years old

Materials: Apples (green, red, yellow); cutting board; knife; napkins; large paper divided in three; red, yellow, green markers

Procedure: Locate all materials. Set up area for group-time. Children and teachers wash hands. Discuss apples: differences, similarities. Draw green, red, and yellow apples on large paper. Cut apples and let each child eat a slice of each color apple. Teacher and/or children graph their favorite apple on chart.

Measuring/Pouring Rice
Developmental Focus: Cognitive

Goal: The children will have an opportunity to explore measuring and pouring.

Age Range: 3 and 4 years old

Materials: sand and water table set up with three tubs, rice, measuring cups and spoons

Procedure: Set up sand and water table with rice in three tubs, measuring cups and spoons in each. Children explore the rice by measuring and pouring. Children discover mathematical concepts by experiential use of materials. Facilitate experience by communicating with child.

Add your own math activity ideas:

_____

_____

_____

_____

_____

_____

_____

_____

_____

SCIENCE ACTIVITIES

Grass Seed Growing on Sponge

Developmental Focus: Cognitive

Goal: The children will have an opportunity to observe grass growing on a sponge.

Age Range: 3 and 4 years old

Materials: tray, grass seed, sponges, squirt bottle with water

Procedure: Assemble all materials on tray. Work with small group to discuss growing grass seed. Children wet sponge with squirt bottle. Children sprinkle ample grass seed on top of sponge and water again. Children observe grass seeds on Science shelf as they begin to grow. Can use children's scissors to cut after seeds grow.

Ice Melt

Developmental Focus: Cognitive

Goal: The children will have an opportunity to explore properties of ice.

Age Range: 3 and 4 years old

Materials: large blocks of ice in tubs, rock salt in small containers, eyedroppers, water dyed with food coloring in small containers (two primary colors)

Procedure: Freeze water in large blocks, or purchase. Locate and set out all materials. Child sprinkles rock salt on ice and uses eyedropper to squirt water. Child observes ice melting and colors mixing. Facilitate experience by discussing observations.

Sorting Seashells

Developmental Focus: Cognitive

Goal: The child will have an opportunity to explore and sort seashells.

Age Range: 3 and 4 years old

Materials: sorting tray with numerous compartments, assortment of seashells (two to three each of various types)

Procedure: Locate all materials. Set up sorting tray with all shells in large compartment. Child takes activity from shelf and sorts shells by type and/or size. Facilitate child's experience by discussing attributes of shells. Child replaces all materials, returns activity to shelf.

Planting Seeds

Developmental Focus: Cognitive

Goal: Children will be allowed to observe the process of plant growth.

Age Range: Appropriate for all ages

Materials: seeds (bean seeds work well), potting soil, individual plastic flower pots (can use Styrofoam™ cups), water, plastic spoons, permanent marking pen

Procedure: Presoak beans for 2 to 3 hours (for quickest growth). Gather materials, set up table outside. Talk to children about seeds. Discuss growing. Child uses spoon to put potting soil in his or her pot. Child places 1 to 2 seeds in the pot, covers with soil. Write child's name on pot. Child waters pot and places in sunny location.

Colors in Nature

Developmental Focus: Cognitive, Social

Goal: The children will experience observing the colors in nature.

Age Range: Appropriate for all ages

Materials: pictures of colors in nature (animals, plants, groundcovers, etc.), toilet paper rolls, stapler, hole punch, yarn

Procedure: Locate and laminate pictures. Gather materials for toilet paper roll "binoculars," assemble with two rolls stapled together, string yarn through holes for neck strap. Set up for group-time. Discuss colors in nature at group-time, show pictures. Divide group into 3 to 4 (with adult)—assign color to observe. Children take nature walk with teachers, observing for "their" color. Facilitate discussion of colors in nature, why certain colors?

Let's Help the Birds!

Developmental Focus: Cognitive, Physical

Goal: To allow the child to provide nesting materials for birds.

Age Range: Appropriate for all ages

Materials: bird nests and/or pictures of bird nests; plastic berry baskets; yarn, thread, string, plastic "grass," tinsel, etc.

Procedure: Locate bird nests/pictures. Tie yarn loop on basket for hanging. Display yarns, threads, etc. on tray. Discuss birds and nest making, show examples. Explain that birds look for materials for their nests. Child pushes yarns, strings, etc. through holes in basket, leaving ends dangling free. Assist children in hanging baskets from trees.

Let's Look It Up!

Developmental Focus: Cognitive, Physical

Goal: To allow the child to discover information about an interest.

Age Range: Appropriate for all ages

Materials: science reference books, science software for computer, variety of insect/bug visiting containers

Procedure: Teacher is always prepared for spontaneous sharing of Science materials. Pull out appropriate reference materials, containers, as needed. Child brings in an insect or butterfly, wants to know about it. Tell child that they will "look it up" together. Facilitate child placing insect in a safe viewing container. Teacher and child look it up together. Teacher and child cooperate to make a sign. Release insect safely.

Hands, Eyes, and Nose Tell Me

Developmental Focus: Cognitive, Physical

Goal: The children will have the opportunity to use their senses.

Age Range: 3 and 4 years old

Materials: sensory table, fresh herbs (basil, mint, dill, etc.), blindfold, large bowls (4)

Procedure: Purchase herbs. Set up sensory table with herbs mixed in together in four bowls (1 for each child). Invite children to the sensory table to explore herbs. Children are invited to sort the herbs by sight. Children are challenged to use the blindfold to sort herbs by feel and smell. Facilitate children's exploration by discussion of herbs and senses.

Plants

Developmental Focus: Cognitive

Goal: Children will plant a terrarium and watch the roots go down while the stem goes up.

Age Range: 3–5

Materials: 2 clear plastic cups, two or three large seeds, such as corn or beans, potting soil, water, tape

Procedure: Put enough dirt in one of the cups to fill it halfway. Place the two seeds on opposite sides against the inner lining of the cup. You should be able to see the seeds through the cup. Pour about 5 teaspoons of water into the cup. Place the second cup upside down on top of the first cup. Tape the edges together and close the gap. Place in a warm environment and watch the roots go down while the seeds go up.

Animals

Developmental Focus: Cognitive

Goal: Children will explore the different feel of animal furs.

Age Range: 3–5

Materials: 3 or 4 swatches of fabric (leather, faux fur, wool), paper bag, pictures of different animals (cow, fox, sheep)

Procedure: Talk with the children about the different animals. Tell them which ones produce what for each of us to wear. Introduce the fabrics to the children. Put each swatch of fabric in the paper bag. Have the children reach inside the bag and guess which piece of fabric matches which animal.

Weather

Developmental Focus: Cognitive

Goal: Children will learn about the weather in the different seasons.

Age Range: 3–5

Materials: paper, magazines to cut, scissors, glue, markers

Procedure: Have the children fold the paper in half and then in half again, creating four squares. Take the marker and trace the lines created by the folds. Label each square with the name of one of the seasons. Look through the magazines and find pictures of items that the children would wear during the four seasons. Look for sweaters, knit hats, light jackets, baseball caps, bathing suits, shorts, long-sleeve shirts, etc. While talking to the children about the temperature during the seasons, have them place their pictures in the right box. After checking over their work, have them glue the pictures into place.

Add your own science activity ideas:

_____

_____

_____

_____

_____

_____

_____

_____

A number of Web sites offer sample lesson plans for teachers. When downloading lesson plans from the Internet or another source, be sure each plan includes:

- Objective or goal of the lesson

- Materials needed

- Directions for the activity

- Appropriate age group

- Developmental appropriateness

Check the Resources section of this manual for a list of Web sites with lesson plans and other free materials for teachers.

BOOKS FOR CHILDREN

Reading aloud is a wonderful gift you can give to children. Through sharing an interesting book, you introduce them to a world they might not otherwise be able to visit. You can travel anywhere you like; you can have experiences that are outside the realm of your current environment; you can participate in wonderful fantasies; you can be saddened, then uplifted.

Children's desire to read and the ability to do so is fostered by being read to as soon as they are born. Even babies can enjoy looking at picture books and hearing simple stories. Preschoolers love to have favorite books read to them repeatedly. As children move into the school years, they can sustain their interest in longer books that are divided into chapters. When they realize the joy that comes from good books, they are more motivated to read on their own.

Many textbooks provide suggestions for setting up reading corners and providing books for children to read by themselves. This section will focus on books that you can read aloud to children in small or large groups. Remember that the more you read, the better you will become at doing so. When the books have been enjoyed in a group setting, add them to the book corner for children to read alone. In addition, teachers often create lending arrangements where children can take home books for their parents to read and then return. Teachers who believe in the importance of reading choose the best of children's literature and involve families in reading.

HOW TO GET CHILDREN TO LISTEN AND WANT MORE

____ Schedule time each day for reading, maybe toward the end of the day when children are tired and will enjoy the inactivity; make sure the setting is comfortable.

_____ Choose books that you also enjoy, perhaps one you read as a child; preview the book before presenting it to the children in case there are passages you want to shorten.

_____ The first time you read a book, state the title and author. Research for interesting facts about the author to share with the children. If there is an illustrator, include that information as well.

_____ If you are reading to a large group, position yourself so that you are slightly higher than the children so that your voice will project more easily.

_____ If you are reading to a small group, sit among them in a more intimate placement, which will draw them to you and the book.

_____ Occasionally stop and ask, "What do you think is going to happen next?"

_____ Read at a pace that allows children to build mental images of the characters or setting; change your pace to match the action of the story: slow your pace and lower your voice during a suspenseful spot and then speed up when the action does.

_____ Allow time for discussion only if children wish to do so. Let them voice fears, ask questions, or share their thoughts about the book. Do not turn it into a quiz or need to interpret the story.

_____ Practice reading aloud, trying to vary your expression or tone of voice.

_____ Create a display of images or information pertaining to the book you are reading. A map will allow children to pinpoint places mentioned in the story. Pictures, charts, or time lines will also add to the display. Objects or foods mentioned in the book add another dimension.

_____ Find a stopping place each day that will create suspense, so that the children are eager to get back to the book the next day.

_____ When you pick up the book the next day, ask if they remember what had happened just before you stopped reading.

WHAT NOT TO DO

____ Don't read a book you do not enjoy; your feelings will be sensed by the children.

____ Don't read a book when it becomes obvious that it was a poor choice; previewing the book before presenting it to the children can minimize these kinds of mistakes.

____ Don't choose a book with which some of the children are already familiar; they may have heard it at home or seen a version on television or the movies.

____ Don't start a book unless you have enough time to read more than a few pages.

____ Don't be fooled by awards. Just because a book has received a national book award does not mean that it is suitable for your particular group of children.

____ Don't impose on the children your own interpretations or reactions to the story. Let them express their own understanding and feelings.

BOOKS

INFANTS AND TODDLERS

10 Minutes till Bedtime, by Peggy Rathman
Scholastic, 1998
Ages 1–6   48 pages
Do you have trouble getting your children to sleep? Try this counting book to help count down to bedtime.

Chicka Chicka Boom Boom, by Bill Martin, Jr. and John
Archambault; illustrated by Lois Ehlert
Simon & Schuster Adult Publishing Group, 1989
Ages Infants–preschool   40 pages
Learn the alphabet with an enticing chant. Pre-algebra skills can be taught as well by following the pattern.

Cookies Week, by Cindy Ward; illustrated by Tomie dePaola
Penguin Putnam Books for Young Readers, 1997
Ages 1–6   32 pages
What does Cookie the cat do throughout the week? An easy way to introduce the days of the week to the young learner.

Good Night Sweet Butterflies, by Dawn Bentley, Heather Cahoon,
and Melanie Gerth
Simon & Schuster Children's, 2003
Ages Infant–preschool   16 pages
Count the beautiful butterflies as you turn the pages of the book. Also begin to identify colors.

Millions of Snowflakes, by Mary McKenna Siddals; illustrated by
Elizabeth Sayles
Houghton Mifflin Company, 1998

Ages Infants–preschool   26 pages
Count the snowflakes with the child as they fall.

PRESCHOOL

Alexander, Who Used to Be Rich Last Sunday, by Judith Viorst
Simon & Schuster Adult Publishing Group, 1980
Ages 4–8   32 pages
Alexander never seems to be lucky and today is not any better.
Learn to count money while laughing at Alexander's mishaps.

Children's World Cookbook, by Angela Wilkes and Fiona Watt;
illustrated by Nadine Wickenden
Scholastic, 2000
Ages 4–12   96 pages
Do you enjoy cooking with your class? These recipes bring diversity
and multiculturalism into your classroom.

From One to One Hundred, by Teri Sloat
Penguin Putnam Books for Young Readers, 1995
Ages 3–6   32 pages
Count from one to one hundred while turning the pages of this
book.

Growing Vegetable Soup, by Lois Ehlert
Harcourt, 1990
Ages 4–6   32 pages
Did you ever wonder if you could grow vegetable soup? Plant a gar-
den with your class or take a trip to a local farm, buy the vegetables
and prepare the soup.

Hanukkah A Counting Book, by Emily Sper
Scholastic, 2003
Ages 3–6   28 pages
Count in English, Hebrew, and Yiddish the days of Hanukkah.

How Many Stars in the Sky?, by Lenny Holt; illustrated by James E.
Ransome
William Morrow & Company, Incorporated, 1996
Ages 4–6   32 pages
A little boy and his dad go on a trip to the country to get a good look
at the stars. How many did they see?

In the Small, Small Pond, by Denise Fleming
Henry Holt & Company, Incorporated, 1998
Ages 3–6   32 pages
What lives in the pond? Turn my pages and discover the underwater world waiting for you.

In the Tall, Tall Grass, by Denise Fleming
Henry Holt & Company, Incorporated, 1995
Ages 3–6   32 pages
Ever wonder what happens when the grass is overgrown? Turn my pages and find out.

Inch by Inch, by Leo Lionni
William Morrow & Company, Incorporated, 1994
Ages 4–8   32 pages
Study beginning measurement, one inch at a time.

Joseph Had a Little Overcoat, by Simms Taback
Viking, 2000
Ages 4–8   32 pages
Do you need a different way to look at recycling? Have fun watching Joseph's coat go from a coat to a button.

Millions of Cats, by Wanda Gag
Penguin Putnam Books for Young Readers, 1977
Ages 4–8   32 pages
An older couple would like to have a cat, but which one? When all is said and done, the most humble cat is the one chosen to live with them.

Planting a Rainbow, by Lois Ehlert
Harcourt, 1992
Ages 3–6   40 pages
Seeds are planted and sprouts appear, but wait, look at the bright colors and the harvest appears.

Round the Garden, by Omri Glaser; illustrated by Byron Glaser and Sandra Higashi
Harry N. Abrams, Inc., 2000
Ages 3–6   34 pages
The water cycle is clearly explained through this fun story.

The Gardener, by Sarah Stewart; illustrated by David Small
Farrar, Straus and Giroux, 2000

Ages 4–8   32 pages
A little girl goes to visit her aunt and uncle for the summer. While there she softens her uncle by planting a garden.

The Grouchy Ladybug by Eric Carle
HarperCollins Children's Books, 1986
Ages 4–6   48 pages
Explore the hours on a clock while a ladybug looks for someone to fight.

The Hershey®'s Kisses Addition Book, by Jerry Pallotta; illustrated by Rob Bolster
Scholastic, 2000
Ages 3–6   32 pages
Learn the concept of one-to-one and counting as well as addition, just by adding that favorite candy, Hershey® Kisses.

The M&M®'s Brand Chocolate Candies Counting Book, by Barbara Barbiere McGrath
Charlesbridge Publishing, 1994
Ages 3–7   32 pages
Do you love M&M®'s? Then teach the children their colors while counting this delicious candy.

The Umbrella, by Jan Brett
Penguin Putnam Books for Young Readers, 2004
Ages 4–8   32 pages
A little boy goes on a walk through the woods and leaves his umbrella. Turn the pages to see who finds it. Have fun counting the animals as they appear.

There Was a Cold Lady Who Swallowed Some Snow, by Lucille Colandro; illustrated by Jared Lee
Scholastic, 2003
Ages 3–6   32 pages
A new twist on the old tune there was an old lady who swallowed a fly. What else will she swallow today? Read to the end for the surprise.

Thunder Cake, by Patricia Polacco
Penguin Putnam Books for Young Readers, 1997
Ages 4–8   32 pages
What do you do when it thunders? You make a thunder cake of course.

SCHOOL AGE

100th Day Worries, by Margery Cuyler; illustrated by Arthur Howard
Simon & Schuster Adult Publishing Group, 1999
Ages 5–8   32 pages
Are you preparing for the 100th day of school? Is one of your assignments to have the children bring in 100 items? Find out how this little girl worries, then handles this project.

Biggest, Strongest, Fastest, by Steve Jenkins
Houghton Mifflin Company, 1997
Ages 5–8   32 pages
Compare the world's animals to everyday items. The children will learn more about the biggest, strongest, fastest animals in the world today.

Caps for Sale, by Esphyr Slobodkina
HarperCollins Children's Books, 1987
Ages 5–7   48 pages
What happens when a cap seller takes a nap? It is fun to have your students act out being the monkeys.

Hershey®'s Kisses Multiplication and Division, by Jerry Pallotta; illustrated by Rob Bolster
Scholastic, 2003
Ages 6–8   32 pages
Describing sets for multiplication can be difficult, but not when you add Hershey® Kisses. Enjoy.

Hershey®'s Milk Chocolate Weights and Measures, by Jerry Pallotta; illustrated by Rob Bolster
Scholastic, 2003
Ages 6–9   32 pages
Have fun while learning about weights and measures while using Hershey®'s chocolate bars.

Less than Zero, by Stuart J. Murphy; illustrated by Frank Remkiewicz
Scholastic, 2003
Age 7   40 pages

Have you ever had trouble explaining a negative number? This book does a great job of following a penguin on his money journey from positive to negative.

Over in the Garden, by Jennifer Ward; illustrated by Kenneth J. Spengler
Scholastic, 2002
Ages 5–7   32 pages
Count the insects and animals in the garden while singing to the tune of "Over in the Meadow." Can you find the hidden numbers?

Parts, by Tedd Arnold
Penguin Putnam Books for Young Readers, 2000
Ages 5–8   32 pages
My body has so many parts. What are they used for and why do I need them?

The Bubble Factory, by Tomie dePaola
Penguin Group, 1996
Ages 5–7   32 pages
Grandpa used to work at the bubble factory. He returns one day to fix the machine and brings his grandchildren. This is entertaining and funny.

The Doorbell Rang, by Pat Hutchins
William Morrow & Company, Incorporated, 1989
Ages 5–8   24 pages
Mom has baked cookies and brother and sister have divided them to eat, but the doorbell rings.

The Hatseller and the Monkeys, by Baba Wague Diakite
Scholastic, 2000
Ages 5–7   30 pages
This is a West African version of *Caps for Sale.* The unique spin is one to be enjoyed.

The Hershey®'s Kisses Subtraction Book, by Jerry Pallotta; illustrated by Rob Bolster
Scholastic, 2002
Ages 6–8   32 pages
Have fun while learning subtraction by using Hershey® Kisses.

The Hershey®'s Milk Chocolate Fractions Book, by Jerry Pallotta;
illustrated by Rob Bolster
Scholastic, 1999
Ages 6–8   32 pages
Explore fractions with chocolate.

The Tiny Seed, by Eric Carle
Simon & Schuster Children's, 1991
Ages 5–8   32 pages
A seed travels to its final resting place and explores many adventures along the way.

DEVELOPMENTALLY APPROPRIATE PRACTICE

NAEYC's first position statement on Developmentally Appropriate Practice had two main motivations:

- The process of accrediting centers required, widely accepted, and specific definitions of what constituted excellent practices in early childhood education.

- There was a proliferation of programs that had inappropriate practices and expectations for their children, largely based on premature academic learning.

The original position statement did enhance the early childhood profession, although it was not received with universal acceptance, so a revised position statement clarified some of the previous misunderstandings and expanded the vision of good practices.

It is important to keep the principles firmly in mind when making professional decisions. It is also important to use the statement in conversations with others regarding appropriate practices. Colleagues, administrators, and family members all have their individual understandings of what to do with young children. It is, therefore, useful for every teacher to have a copy of the position statement. In a conversation, you can use the position statement to replace the idea of personal opinions with the weight of the professional body of knowledge. The complete statement, Developmentally Appropriate Practice in Early Childhood Programs, Revised Edition (1997, NAEYC), can be found at http://www.naeyc.org click on Information About NAEYC>Position Statements>Developmentally Appropriate Practice. The introduction follows:

DEVELOPMENTALLY APPROPRIATE PRACTICE IN EARLY CHILDHOOD PROGRAMS SERVING CHILDREN FROM BIRTH THROUGH AGE 8

A Position Statement for the National Association for the Education of Young Children

Adopted July 1996

This statement defines and describes principles of developmentally appropriate practice in early childhood programs for administrators, teachers, parents, policy-makers, and others who make decisions about the care and education of young children. An early childhood program is any group program in a center, school, or other facility that serves children from birth through age eight. Early childhood programs include child care centers, family child care homes, private and public preschools, kindergartens, and primary-grade schools.

The early childhood profession is responsible for establishing and promoting standards of high-quality, professional practice in early childhood programs. These standards must reflect current knowledge and shared beliefs about what constitutes high-quality, developmentally appropriate early childhood education in the context within which services are delivered.

GUIDELINES FOR DEVELOPMENTALLY APPROPRIATE PRACTICE

NAEYC's DAP guidelines can be implemented in your daily work with children:

CREATE A CARING ENVIRONMENT AMONG CHILDREN AND ADULTS

Children:

- learn personal responsibility
- develop constructive relationships with others
- respect individual and cultural differences

Adults:

- get to know each child, taking into account individual differences and developmental level
- adjust the pace and content of the curriculum so that children can be successful most of the time
- bring each child's culture and language into the setting
- expect children to be tolerant of others' differences

THE CURRICULUM AND SCHEDULE ALLOW CHILDREN TO SELECT AND INITIATE THEIR OWN ACTIVITIES

Children:

- learn through active involvement in a variety of learning experiences
- build independence by taking on increasing responsibilities
- initiate their own activities to follow their interests

83

Adults:

- provide a variety of materials and activities that are concrete and real

- provide a variety of work places and spaces

- arrange the environment so that children can work alone or in groups

- extend children's learning by posing problems, asking thought-provoking questions

- add complexity to tasks as needed

- model, demonstrate, and provide information so children can progress in their learning

THE PROGRAM IS ORGANIZED AND INTEGRATED SO THAT CHILDREN DEVELOP A DEEPER UNDERSTANDING OF KEY CONCEPTS AND SKILLS

Children:

- engage in activities that reflect their current interests

- plan and predict outcomes of their research

- share information and knowledge with others

Adults:

- plan related activities and experiences that broaden children's knowledge and skills

- design curriculum to foster important skills like literacy and numeracy

- adapt instruction for children who are ahead or behind age-appropriate expectations

- plan curriculum so that children achieve important developmental goals

ACTIVITIES AND EXPERIENCES HELP CHILDREN DEVELOP A POSITIVE SELF-IMAGE WITHIN A DEMOCRATIC COMMUNITY

Children:

- learn through reading books about other cultures

- read about current events and discuss how these relate to different cultures

- accept differences among their peers, including children with disabilities

Adults:

- provide culturally and non-sexist activities and materials that foster children's self-identity

- design the learning environment so children can learn new skills while using their native language

- allow children to demonstrate their learning using their own language

ACTIVITIES AND EXPERIENCES DEVELOP CHILDREN'S AWARENESS OF THE IMPORTANCE OF COMMUNITY INVOLVEMENT

Children:

- are ready and eager to learn about the world outside their immediate environment

- are open to considering different ways of thinking or doing things

- can benefit from contact with others outside their homes or child care setting

Adults:

- encourage awareness of the community at large

- plan experiences in facilities within the community

- bring outside resources and volunteers into the child care setting

- encourage children to plan their involvement based on their own interests.

PROFESSIONAL ORGANIZATIONS

When looking to further your development, a professional organization is a great place to start. There are several organizations, some of which even have state or local affiliates.

National Association for the Education of Young Children (NAEYC)
1509 16th Street, NW
Washington, DC 20036
800-424-2460
http://www.naeyc.org
Email membership@naeyc.org

Specific membership benefits:
Comprehensive Members receive all the benefits of Regular membership described below plus annually receive five or six books immediately after their release by NAEYC.

Regular and Student Members receive:

- Six issues of *Young Children,* which includes timely articles on pertinent issues, as well as suggestions and strategies for enhancing children's learning

- Reduced registration fees at NAEYC-sponsored local and national conferences and seminars

- Discounted prices on hundreds of books, videos, brochures, and posters from NAEYC's extensive catalog of materials

- Access to the *Members Only* Web site, including links to additional resources and chat sites for communication with other professionals

National Association of Child Care Professionals (NACCP)
P.O. Box 90723
Austin, TX 78709
800-537-1118
www.naccp.org

Specific membership benefits:
Management Tools of the Trade™
Your membership provides complete and FREE access (a $79 value) to these effective management tools that provide technical assistance in human resource management. In addition, members will receive NACCP's quarterly trade journals, *Professional Connections©*, *Teamwork©*, and *Caring for Your Children©*, to help you stay on top of hot issues in child care. Each edition also includes a Tool of the Trade™.

National Child Care Association (NCCA)
1016 Rosser Street
Conyers, GA 30012
800-543-7161
http://www.nccanet.org

Specific membership benefits:

- As the only recognized voice in Washington, DC, NCCA has great influence on our legislators

- Professional development opportunities are available

Association for Education International (ACEI)
The Olney Professional Building
17904 Georgia Avenue, Suite 215
Olney, MD 20832
Phone: 800-423-2563 or 301-570-2122
Fax: 301-570-2212
http://www.acei.org

ACEI is an international organization dedicated to promoting the best educational practices throughout the world.

Specific membership benefits:

- Workshops and travel/study tours abroad

- Four issues per year of the journal *Childhood Education* and the *Journal of Research in Childhood Education*

- Hundreds of resources for parents and teachers, including books, pamphlets, audiotapes, and videotapes

National AfterSchool Association (NAA)
1137 Washington Street
Boston, MA 02124
Phone: 617-298-5012
Fax: 617-298-5022
http://www.naaweb.org

NAA is a national organization dedicated to providing information, technical assistance, and resources concerning children in out-of-school programs. Members include teachers, policy makers, and administrators representing all public, private, and community-based sectors of after-school programs.

Specific membership benefits:

- A subscription to the NAA journal, *School-Age Review*

- A companion membership in state affiliates

- Discounts on NAA publications and products

- Discount on NAA annual conference registration

- Opportunity to be an NAA accreditation endorser

- Public policy representatives in Washington, DC

Other organizations to contact:

The Children's Defense Fund
25 E. Street NW
Washington, DC 20001
202-628-8787
http://www.childrensdefense.org

National Association for Family Child Care
P.O. Box 10373
Des Moines, IA 50306
800-359-3817
http://www.nafcc.org
Journal: *The National Perspective*

National Black Child Development Institute
1023 15th Avenue NW
Washington, DC 20002
202-833-2220
http://www.nbcdi.org

National Head Start Association
1651 Prince Street
Alexandria, VA 22314
703-739-0875
http://www.nhsa.org
Journal: *Children and Families*

International Society for the Prevention of Child Abuse and Neglect
25 W. 560 Geneva Road, Suite L2C
Carol Stream, IL 60188
630-221-1311
http://www.ispcan.org
Journal: *Child Abuse and Neglect: The International Journal*

Council for Exceptional Children
1110 N. Glebe Road, Suite 300
Arlington, VA 22201
888-CEC-SPED
http://www.cec.sped.org
Journal: *CEC Today*

National Association for Bilingual Education
Union Center Plaza
810 First Street, NE
Washington, DC 20002
http://www.nabe.org
Journal: *NABE Journal of Research and Practice*

International Reading Association
800 Barksdale Road
P.O. Box 8139
Newark, DE 19714
800-336–READ
http://www.reading.org
Journal: *The Reading Teacher*

National Education Organization (NEA)
1201 16th Street NW
Washington, DC 20036
202-833-4000
http://www.nea.org
Journals: *Works4Me* and *NEA Focus,* by on-line subscription

Zero to Three: National Center for Infants, Toddlers, and Families
2000 M. Street NW, Suite 200
Washington, DC 20036
202-638-1144
http://www.zerotothree.org
Journal: *Zero to Three*

RESOURCES

BOOKS

Brown, S. E. (1981). *Bubbles, rainbows and worms.* Mt. Ranier, MD: Gryphon House.

Charlesworth, R. (2005). *Experiences in math for young children* (5th ed.). Clifton Park, NY: Thomson Delmar Learning.

Charlesworth, R. (2005). *Exploring science in early childhood education* (4th ed.). Clifton Park, NY: Thomson Delmar Learning.

Colker, L. J. (2005). *The cooking book.* Washington, DC: NAEYC.

Feely, J. (1994). *Science at play.* Lincolnshire, IL: Learning Resources.

Gold-Dworkin, H. (2000). *Exploring light and color.* New York: McGraw-Hill.

Gold-Dworkin, H. (2000). *Fun with mixing and chemistry.* New York: McGraw-Hill.

Gold-Dworkin, H. (2000). *Fun with water and bubbles.* New York: McGraw-Hill.

Gold-Dworkin, H. (2000). *Learning about the changing seasons.* New York: McGraw-Hill.

Gold-Dworkin, H. (2000). *Learning about the way things move.* New York: McGraw-Hill.

Green, M. D. (1996). *474 Science activities for young children.* Clifton Park, NY: Thomson Delmar Learning.

Hayes, M. A. (1986). *Think it through.* Bridgeport, CT: First Teacher Press.

Herr, J., Larson, Y. L., & Tennyson-Grimm, D. (2004). *Teacher made materials that really teach!* Clifton Park, NY: Thomson Delmar Learning.

Kiernan, D. (2001) *Great graphs, charts & tables that build real-life math skills.* New York:Scholastic.

Martin, D. J. (2001). *Constructing early childhood science.* Clifton Park, NY: Thomson Delmar Learning.

Matricardi, J., & McLarty, J. (2005). *Math activities a to z.* Clifton Park, NY: Thomson Delmar Learning.

Matricardi, J., & McLarty, J. (2005). *Science activities a to z.* Clifton Park, NY: Thomson Delmar Learning.

Mayesky, M. (2006). *Creative activities for young children,* (8th ed.). Clifton Park, NY: Thomson Delmar Learning.

Overholt, J. L., White-Holtz, J., & Dickson, S. (1999). *Big math activities for young children.* Clifton Park, NY: Thomson Delmar Learning.

Prairie, A. P. (2005). *Inquiry into math, science, and technology: For teaching young children.* Clifton Park, NY: Thomson Delmar Learning.

Sisson, E. A. (1982). *Nature with children of all ages.* New York: Prentice Hall.

White, N. (1991). *52 science centers.* New York: Newbridge Communications.

INTERNET RESOURCES

ABC Teach
http://www.abcteach.com
Good sources for play activities, lesson plans, outdoor activities, and center equipment.

A to Z Teacher Stuff
http://www.atozteacherstuff.com/
Teachers can tour this site to find lesson plans and resources to conduct classroom activities.

Bill Nye
http://www.nyelabs.com
A fun way to explore science with the popular Bill Nye the Science Guy.

Birdcam

http://www.kodak.com/

Once in the site, search for the birdcam. Realistic pictures of birds in a variety of settings with information about the bird in the picture are available on this Web site.

BrainPop

http://www.brainpop.com

A great site for older children. Parts of the site are free and parts require registration. A wide variety of topics are available to explore.

Cloud Bursts

http://pals.agron.iastate.edu/

Pictures of clouds are abundant on this site. It is good for all ages. Once on the site click the "Cool Clouds" button.

Core Knowledge

http://www.coreknowledge.org/

What do I teach? A question often asked by many teachers, preschool teachers, too. This site opens the door to the Core Knowledge Curriculum. Many states are using this to drive curriculum development. This site is a helpful resource.

Counting Game

http://home.earthlink.net/

A fun way to have children count and play on the computer. It is not timed, but moves at the children's speed. You will need to search the site for the counting game.

Early Education

http://www.earlyeducation.org/

Turn to this site for the latest trends in preschool education.

Enchanted Learning

http://www.enchantedlearning.com/

Looking for different theme ideas, this site explores astronomy, foreign languages, and the Olympics.

Everything Preschool

http://www.everythingpreschool.com/

This is another resource for lesson plan and theme ideas.

Exploratorium

http://www.exploratorium.org

A museum sponsored site with unique pictures and lots of information.

Family Education Network

http://www.teachervision.fen.com/

This site is for families and teachers to learn more about how to interact with their children.

First School.ws Preschool Activities

http://www.first-school.ws/

When looking for fun ways to explore color and its magic check out this site.

Helping Your Children Learn Math

http://www.ed.gov/

This site gives parents and teachers ideas about how to help children learn math by specific topic areas. Search the site for publications related to math activities.

Hummingbird Ed

http://www.hummingbirded.com

Looking for a good resource for ideas. Check this site out.

Kids Planet

http://www.kidsplanet.org

Games, teacher resources, and information await the learner as they explore the world of science.

Let's Do Math

http://www.ed.gov/

Everyday lessons to do at home, the grocery store, or in the car with your children. Similar to the other site listed above. Search for publications, parents, then learning partners.

Lesson Planz.com

http://lessonplanz.com/

Everything from literacy to science can be found here. Another lesson plan site.

MAD Scientist

http://www.madsci.org

Science experiments await you as you travel through this magical scientific journey.

Mailbox Magazine

http://www.theeducationcenter.com/

Explore this site for fun lesson plans, bulletin boards, and theme ideas as you plan across the curriculum.

National Zoo

http://www.si.edu/

Walk through the national zoo, by playing BINGO, going on a scavenger hunt, or just researching your favorite animal. Under Smithsonian Museums click on the National Zoo link.

North Carolina Ag in the Classroom

http://www.ncagintheclassroom.com/statewide.htm

This site has many materials available for download, including a four-week unit on Ag in the Classroom.

PBS Kids

http://pbskids.org/

PBS Kids contains several links to their programs' Web sites. These Web sites provide games, stories, and related activities to keep learning fun.

Pre-K Smarties

http://www.preksmarties.com

An educational resource for parents that will answer questions and give guidance on hot topics.

Preschool Education

http://www.preschooleducation.com/

This site is the parent site to ask the preschool teacher, preschool printables, and preschool coloring book. It gives information and provides art for teachers to download to create flannelboards and games. Be careful not to use the downloads for the children to color.

Preschool Express

http://www.preschoolexpress.com/

Month by month activities are available here.

Preschool Power

http://www.preschoolpower.com

Articles, activities and ideas for parents and teachers of young children.

Preschool Rainbow

http://www.preschoolrainbow.org/

This site is theme based with teacher input. Some downloads are restricted to members only. Don't let that hinder your visits, there are many that are free.

Preschool by Stormie

http://www.preschoolbystormie.com

This site provides curriculum ideas. Check out the links to shape figures.

Preschool Zone

http://www.preschoolzone.com/

This site has information on preschool news from around the world as well as lesson plan ideas.

Read Aloud Resources

http://www.read2kids.org/

Literacy is a hot topic. This site gives parents and teachers tips on how to read to kids, where to read to kids, and what to read to kids.

Reeko's Mad Scientist Lab

http://www.spartechsoftware.com/

A wealth of science experiments and projects for kids of all ages, parents included, too. To access click on the link to Reeko's Mad Scientist Lab Web site.

Saint Patrick's Day Graph

http://www.tooter4kids.com/

Have fun using a child's favorite cereal to teach a graphing concept. Do a site search for lucky charms.

San Diego Zoo

http://www.sandiegozoo.org

Walk through the zoo, by visiting the animals, researching your favorite animal, or interviewing a zookeeper.

Sanford-Art Adventures

http://www.sanford-artadventres.com

Resources for creative individuals from beginners to advanced.

Scholastic

http://www.scholastic.com/

This is more than a bookseller. This site has activities and ideas for both teachers and parents as well as fun activities for kids.

Sesame Street

http://www.sesameworkshop.org/

This site is a nonprofit organization linked to the Sesame Street characters. The children can have learning to draw and color with their friends.

Space Weather

http://www.sec.noaa.gov

Explore the weather out in space every day all day. What is the weather today?

Stormy Weather

http://www.spc.noaa.gov

Predict storms, see weather reports from across the country, and map a storm on this Web site.

Teaching K-8

http://www.TeachingK-8.com

Excellent source for teacher resources.

The Education Place

http://www.eduplace.com

A resource for theme ideas to complete those lesson plans.

The Idea Box

http://www.theideabox.com/

Looking for new ideas, check this site out.

Tiny Planets

http://www.tinyplanets.com

Through different characters in outer space, the children can play games, mix colors, and tour outer space.

Very Best Kids

http://www.VeryBestKids.com

Source for creative activities across the curriculum.

Worst Weather

http://www.mountwashington.org

Learn all about Mount Washington and its weather by exploring this site. Fun facts are sure to be found.

Zero to Three

http://www.zerotothree.org/

This Web site provides information specific to infants and toddlers.

CASE STUDIES

These are a few brief scenarios and possible solutions to problems you may encounter in your classroom.

Science is not valued in your center. The director tells you that all she wants you to do is keep the fish alive in the aquarium.

What would your response be?
Possible solutions:

- Explain to the director that you would like to introduce the children to nature by using magnifying glasses.

- Ask for permission to go on a nature walk.

- Bring nature indoors and do crayon rubbings and sensory explorations.

A parent wants their child to be able to count to 20 in the two year old room and know the difference between the monetary coins.

What would your response be?
Possible solutions:

- Counting by rote is just that, pure memorization. I am working on number meanings. Right now we are up to three.

- The use of coins in the classroom at this time would not be safe. The children are still exploring by putting things in their mouth. I will watch for signs of readiness and keep that in mind for future lessons.

- Keep counting with your child. Count the plates on the table, the cans of vegetables in the grocery cart, the number of cars that go by, the time it takes for the light to turn green, and the number of squirrels in the trees. Before you know it they will be counting to 20.

A parent comes to complain that her child tells her she only puts together puzzles all day. Do you not watch her and make her go to other areas of the room?

What would your response be?
Possible solutions:

- I see your concern, but let me assure you, many skills are learned in the puzzle corner. Puzzles are a start to pre-reading skills, they draw the child's attention to shape and pattern, and they are used to sort by characteristics. In other words, puzzles are a very valuable part of each child's day.

- Fine motor skills are developed by putting together puzzles. Your child can now put together puzzles with 15 pieces.

Math and Science are often neglected areas of the early childhood classroom. Many teachers are not comfortable with their own skills in this area or did not like these subjects while in school so they tend to avoid them in their class. One thing I tell my classes when the semester starts is to forget your past. We are here to have fun and explore the world around us. We will go on nature walks, build with Legos®, cook, and create art. I enjoy making pattern necklaces, doing a cooperative Lego® town, and cooking with my classes. The more comfortable I can make the teachers with their skills, the more likely they will include them in their weekly themes.

- When going on a nature walk, I guide my students through a game of Nature BINGO. I give each student a card with 25 squares. In each square, I put an item I hope to see while on our walk (cloud, sun, bird nest, dandelion, leaf, bark, etc.) When making the cards, I put the 25 items in different squares. I do not make 25 different cards, just one, and the one who fills the entire card is the winner.

- A Lego® town is a cooperative activity. I have a box filled with Legos® and I walk around the classroom placing handfuls of Legos® on each table. I ask the students to use all of their Legos® to build something. When finished, they need to attach their creation to another table's creation and so on until all the Legos® have been attached to each other. This teaches the students about spatial relationships.

- Cooking is a great way to "measure" your students' math skills. Bring in your favorite recipe for cookies and the ingredients to double the recipe. You could have the students bring in the ingredients. Have the students rewrite the recipe doubled and halved. Then present the ingredients and have them measure, mix, and bake the cookies. Enjoy.

Often I show them how easy science can be with recyclables. We can make bird feeders out of two-liter bottles, a sorting game out of a junk drawer, and a matching game out of rinsed cans. Science and Math go together and I think trying to separate them is what causes much of the confusion. Revisit the manipulatives corner and re-think the supplies. Puzzles, matching, lotto, file folder games, mag-nifying glasses, animals, and plants all belong here. Put them there and watch the children's imagination grow and yours as well as you explore the world around you with science and math.

- To make a bird feeder out of a two-liter bottle, rinse the bottle. Poke a hole through the top. Attach a string by threading it through the hole and then tying a knot on the inside of the cap. Cut a large square out of the side of the bottle. Run a popsicle stick through the bottle, just below the square opening (for the bird to sit). Fill with bird seed and hang in a tree.

- Make a matching game out of rinsed soup cans. Rinse the can and tape the edge with either duct tape or electrical tape. Peel off the label. Draw a design on a strip of paper large enough to fit around the can. Repeat the design on another strip of paper the same size. Tape one to the can and cut the other one apart. Glue a magnet onto the back of each piece and have the children match the pieces to the complete design.

Science is becoming a new focus in the classroom as it will now be tested along with the other standard subjects of reading, writing, and math. Science therefore needs equal time in the classroom. Watch the news, read the newspaper, talk to the children, and be-gin your exploration with what is happening in the world or in their minds. Children want to be included in the discovery and inquiry process, let them lead the lessons while you guide. Also, remember that Science does not need to be taught from page one to the end. Jump around and have fun.

Topics you may want to include as you begin are:
- plants—seeds, parts of a plant, the life cycle of the plant
- animals—zoo, farm, ocean, forest, jungle

- water—bubbles, floating, sinking, liquid, solid, gas

- magnets—attraction, repelling

- electricity—complete circuit, incomplete circuits

- color—create colors, change colors, tints, hues

- space—planets, stars, moon, gravity

- weather—sun, rain, snow, fog, temperature, seasons, clothing

ETHICS

"The NAEYC Code of Ethical Conduct offers guidelines for responsible behavior and sets forth a common basis for resolving the principle dilemmas encountered in early childhood care and education." (This is a quote from Feeney, S. & Freeman, N. K. (1999). *Ethics and the Early Childhood Educator: Using the NAEYC Code.* Washington, DC: NAEYC.) Some of the following main points from that document follow; they should guide you in reacting to and managing the common situations you will encounter in your work with children, parents, and your colleagues.

Ethical Responsibilities to Children

Your primary responsibility as a caregiver is to provide a safe, nurturing, and responsive environment for children. In doing so, each child's uniqueness must be respected.

Caregivers and teachers:

- remain current in their knowledge of requirements for children's care and education

- recognize each child's unique characteristics and needs

- include children with disabilities and provide access to support services as needed

- above all else, adults shall not harm any child

- seek input from families and other professionals in order to maximize the potential of every child to benefit from the program

Ethical Responsibilities to Families

Caregivers share mutual responsibility for children's development with parents or any others who are involved with the children. There must be a collaborative relationship between home and school.

Caregivers:

_____ foster a relationship of mutual trust with parents

_____ respect families' culture, language, and child-rearing decisions

_____ help families improve child-rearing skills and their understanding of their children's development

_____ allow parents to have access to their children's program setting

_____ inform parents and involve them in policy decisions when it is appropriate

_____ involve families in important decisions concerning their children

_____ maintain confidentiality and respect parents' rights to privacy

_____ use community resources and services that can support families

Ethical Responsibilities to Colleagues

The main focus of this section is on establishing a caring and cooperative workplace in which each person is respected. Your main responsibility is to establish professional relationships that support productive work and meet professional needs.

Staff members:

_____ develop relationships of respect, trust, and cooperation

_____ make full use of the expertise and training of all staff members

_____ have working conditions that are safe and supportive and based on written personnel policies

_____ are supported in efforts to meet professional needs and in professional development

_____ will be informed of areas where they do not meet program standards and are assisted in improving

Responsibility to Community and Society

Every child care facility operates within a community made up of families and other institutions whose main concern is the welfare of children. It is important that the program meets the needs of the community and cooperates with other agencies.

The child care program will:

_____ provide the community with high quality, developmentally appropriate care for children

_____ be sensitive to cultural differences among the children's families

_____ support policies and laws that benefit children and families

_____ communicate openly about the kinds of services offered

_____ hire only persons who are competent

_____ report unethical behavior of a coworker or supervisor